The
LITTLE
MONEY
Bible

Also by Stuart Wilde

The LITTLE MONEY Bible

The Ten Laws of Abundance

Stuart Wilde

HAY HOUSE, INC.

Carlsbad, California • New York City
London • Sydney • Johannesburg
Vancouver • Hong Kong • New Delhi

Published and distributed in the United States by: Hay House, Inc.: www.hayhouse.com • *Published and distributed in Australia by:* Hay House Australia Pty. Ltd.: www.hayhouse.com.au • *Published and distributed in the United Kingdom by:* Hay House UK, Ltd.: www.hayhouse.co.uk • *Published and distributed in the Republic of South Africa by:* Hay House SA (Pty), Ltd.: www.hayhouse.co.za • *Distributed in Canada by:* Raincoast: www.raincoast.com • *Published in India by:* Hay House Publishers India: www.hayhouse.co.in

Edited by: Anna Scott and Jill Kramer
Designed by: Wendy Lutge

Library of Congress Cataloging-in-Publication Data

Wilde, Stuart
    The little money Bible / Stuart Wilde.
        p. cm.
    ISBN 1-56170-393-1 (hardcover) • 1-56170-829-1 (tradepaper)
        1. Wealth—Religious aspects—Buddhism, Christianity.   2. Wilde, Stuart,
    1946–   . I. Title.
    BR115.W4W46   1998
    241'.68—dc21   98-15929
                                                                              CIP

ISBN 13: 978-1-56170-829-1
ISBN 10: 1-56170-829-1

11 10 09 08   12 11 10 9
1st printing, May 1998
9th printing, April 2008

Printed in the United States of America

Contents

The Ten Laws of Abundance

Introduction

We live in challenging times—markets have become more volatile, and governments are ever more regulatory and grasping over their citizens' wealth. It's time to review the laws of money. In such changing conditions, it's easy to lose sight of the fact that we live in a very abundant world, that the laws of money and flow are eternal and natural, and that nothing has really changed; abundance is our birthright.

Here, in this little book, I will reiterate the main laws and principles from my other books on abundance—*The Trick to Money Is Having Some* and *Life Was Never Meant to Be a Struggle*—and encapsulate them for a fast and easy read. These are the laws of money; they serve to remind us how to align effortlessly with flow and abundance.

Money is energy. Your life is energy. You're a physical body, a personality formed from a collection of memories. But what you are in the end is a *feeling*. That feeling has a spiritual identity—it is your soul.

Money is also a feeling: a feeling of wealth, security, flow, and success. Sometimes money can be a feeling of importance and specialness, a feeling of power. Throughout history, philosophers and the great religious leaders have taught that there is a divine abundance, which ebbs and flows through our lives as the seasons do.

We are loved and provided for. Money is just a symbol of the infinite goodness, the compassion that gave us life. We intrinsically know how to manage on the physical plane; the knowing is God-given and natural.

In these pages, I lay out the "Ten Laws of Abundance." This is not a "Rah! Rah! Up and at 'em, get-your-act-together" book. Instead, I look at the psychological aspects of aligning to money. But you'll also find the deeper, metaphysical secrets of abundance laid out here—the inner game, as some call it. They are the subtleties known only to some—subtleties usually overlooked because they are not immediately obvious.

We each have to search within to comprehend the ebb and flow of money in our lives. It is one of the great spiritual lessons of the earth-plane—as are physical balance, love and compassion, interpersonal relationships, and the other experiences we collect in life.

Money is important—first, because obviously we have to eat. Second, because as divine spirits, we get a free body, and we're spiritually required to take that body around the earth-plane to collect life's experiences.

Mobility is important; it grants you the wherewithal to delve deep within yourself, to pull out your true power. From that personal power flows all the money you'll ever need. At the end of your life, with all its triumphs and all its beauty, you are just the collection of memories you managed to acquire. Those memories make up your spiritual identity—your soul, expressed as a sacred, infinite feeling. And that composite feeling, the story of your life, is the real you. It is eternal, for within it is the divine spark of God.

Over the centuries, money has gotten a bad rap. It has been associated with corruption and the misuse of power. The perception grew that somehow the rich deprived the poor, and that if you became wealthy, you disconnected yourself from love, goodness, and the God Force.

That is not necessarily so. I genuinely believe you can be rich and spiritual, and that with your abundance you can create love and compassion—using your wealth to help others strengthen themselves so they might also accumulate money— each one spreading his or her wealth around so that everyone can collect the experiences they need to become proficient in life's ways, to become fully transcendent and wise.

In John Randolph Price's wonderful little volume, *The Abundance Book*, he cleverly reminds us that all the philosophies and religious systems of the Ancients included the concept of self-sufficiency—that the ideas of harmony, peace, and abundance are common to all cultures. Price quotes nine excerpts from the Bible: abundance affirmations such as "Beloved, I wish above all things that thou mayest prosper," and "...Thou shalt remember the Lord thy God, for it is He that giveth thee the power to get wealth."

Most of us don't remember these; we only remember that "money is the root of all evil." But the actual quotation is "The *love* of money is the root of all evil." Money of itself is a symbol of appreciation, a gesture of goodwill and compassion. It's only the negative emotions around money that are evil: greed, avarice, an obsession with power, and so on.

Money is neutral; it's only a solidified form of energy (light), and light, of course, is also neutral—it can illuminate a church or cast shadows in a torture chamber. In the early Christian era, the church sought to control people. The ideas of self-sufficiency and the oneness of all things were edited out of the scriptures and religious teachings. Self-empowerment and independence were considered threats to religious authority and the feudal control of common people. But times have changed.

Price mentions in his booklet that the Transcendental Movement has, in the period of just over one hundred years or so, reclaimed the concepts of abundance, harmony, and the oneness of life. It began with Ralph Waldo Emerson and the early Theosophists; then on via Mary Baker Eddy, the founder of Christian Science, and those who formed the New Thought Movement—each one helping to reestablish the spirituality of self-empowerment.

Price also points out that the idea of spiritual empowerment of the individual was carried from tentative beginnings to a greater and greater acceptance, finally emerging as a great spiritual light. This has been carried through the decades into this century via important teachers such as Charles and Myrtle Fillmore (Unity), Nona Brooks (Divine Science), and, of course, Ernest Holmes (Religious Science).

It was these courageous forerunners who allowed the New Age of Enlightenment to take hold and New Thought to pervade our modern societies. The ideas of self-sufficiency, abundance, and enlightenment are no longer threatening to many. People now realize that they are responsible for their own empowerment. They see that taking responsibility is a spiritual act; it allows each one the freedom to become more.

For that to happen, people have to be brave; they have to grasp the idea that they can control their lives. Accepting responsibility is an uncomfortable thing, for within that idea is the birth of the true individual. It's the only solution to our societies' problems. Expecting someone else to fix our lives is silly; in the end we need six billion individual fixes.

In the past, we were manipulated and shamed into believing that the individual was not important, that all power and control over our lives should be handed over to the authorities—who would act as custodians of the collective good. Watching those characters manage the collective good for their own ends, often to the detriment of ordinary people, caused many to wonder if the philosophy of such disempowerment actually worked. The collective good became known, amusingly, I think, as the Public Interest—which turned out to be anything that suited the leaders of our spiritual, financial, and political status quo.

The endless manipulation and control of our societies was sold as an idea that is holy and good. After all, who could argue against the Public Interest? However, the idea that some brainless drone in a pinstripe suit, on a massive power trip, can tell you what color to paint your front door hasn't generated much interest from the general public.

On the religious/spiritual front, we were sold the idea that we needed the authorities to intercede with God on our behalf. It has taken us over a thousand years to realize that this idea is rather silly and that we can have a little chat with God anytime we like, without asking permission or hiring a spokesman. What's cool about the modern Christian churches is that they don't say you have to go through them to get to God. Instead, they teach people to empower themselves. Of course, the concepts of taking responsibility and empowering yourself, and granting yourself the freedom to guide your own spiritual destiny are radical ideas that are still taking shape.

Look at our Western democracies. In theory, they are free; but in reality, what freedoms do we have? There are millions of rules that empower the authorities, while milking the citizens and controlling every aspect of our lives. I often say that you are free as long as you don't want to do anything. The minute you get a creative moneymaking idea, the political system jumps in with you. In true Mafia style, they become your silent partners. You get the work and the risk, and they effortlessly get a large chunk of the reward, while placing a hundred hurdles in your way.

In Europe, where institutional control was invented for the most part, self-empowerment still isn't considered cool. The idea that you might want to make money, become abundant, and direct your life is still regarded as brutal, egotistical, and rather nasty. Anyone headed in such a direction will have to plow through endless negative waves of antagonistic opinion. They will have to be brave and face the manipulators, who heap shame and ridicule on anyone who seeks to break out of the straitjacket of the old mind-set.

Still, we haven't lost heart. Our time has come, and the rules of money are simple. It's not too hard to quietly thread your way through the morass of nonsense, to still make it and become free. Millions of energetic people have done it, in spite of the system. The new idea is here: Control is very old-fashioned, and our societies will change gradually as people come to see that the old system just doesn't work.

I think the pioneer spirit of Americans has allowed them to embrace the idea of individuality more readily. People in America are more free; they are not so tied to the memory of ancient feudal systems. As a result, the New Thought has gained ground in America, and individuals can strive for abundance, liberty, and mobility without feeling bad about it. People want to be free; they want to experience life to the fullest without having to subjugate themselves to restrictive institutional controls. It stands to reason.

Yet even in America, a push-pull process has been going on for 50 years between the old-style forces of control and the new ideas that seek to liberate. The advantage Americans have is that they aren't subjected to the shame inflicted on ordinary Europeans who seek self-empowerment and wealth. That fact allowed progressive religious leaders such as Ernest Holmes to form Christian churches that taught self-empowerment.

These progressive modern churches have radically challenged the old ideas. They, more than anything else, have given birth to the Age of Enlightenment. Throw in the hippies, flower power, and the New Age movement, and suddenly great swaths of the population are thinking differently. Each one is pushing against the Thought Police, those who seek to disempower and impoverish us by controlling, marginalizing, and ridiculing alternative ideas.

John Randolph Price says, "It is now estimated that at least 25 percent of America is involved, in some measure, with what is considered Esoteric Philosophy or New Thought religion.

And right in the mainstream of this consciousness is the Truth that God is boundless wealth, and as expressions of the Infinite we have an abundant inheritance."

In the time frame of history, these ideas are brand new, and yet they have swept America like wildfire and spread from there across the Western world. The concept of abundance and self-reliance is being given a new image. Teachers have carried out the new idea, saying that it's okay for individuals to take control of their lives, and wealth when used sensibly is spiritual, desirable, and above all natural.

That is not to say that poverty is necessarily unnatural, for some are born into difficult situations where they lack opportunity or education. Yet we all can rise, no matter how humble our origins, for money is energy. And generating energy requires nothing except enthusiasm.

We should also remember that the inability to align to money and abundance is not a misfortune. Nor is it necessarily bad luck, or a sad karma you've been shouldered with. More often than not, a lack of money is the result of errors in the fine-tuning of the buttons and knobs that make up the *real* you and your grand plan.

The difference between the tramp and the millionaire is an almost imperceptible shift in consciousness and vitality. You too can make an upward shift simply and easily. You can learn to be more open, and place yourself in the flow while learning the subtle laws of money and abundance, so that life's opportunities come to you more naturally. It's all part of your spiritual journey.

That is not to say that people who are very rich are necessarily very spiritual—some are naturally adapted to the marketplace of life. However, in order to be a complete, whole, divine being, with a bag full of memories and experiences, you may need to make the adjustments.

So here are the Ten Laws of Abundance, along with the underlying metaphysics and a brief discussion on what action you might take. I trust that I can remind you of the things you already know, bring to you perceptions you may have missed, and urge you to take certain actions, so you can step into the prosperity and security that is a natural part of our human evolution.

Yes, the rules and regulations of life can make things a bit harder, but if you have the knowledge, it becomes easy once more. By the end of this little book, I hope I will have convinced you of that.

In addition, I hope you will see that in some instances, compassion can be described as the manifestation of love in action. And that money is, in part, the fuel by which you express a greater compassion—by transcending a poor self-image, loving yourself, being there for others; and by being grateful for the immense gift that has been bestowed upon you, the first and greatest gift you will ever receive—the gift of life.

—ᜋ—

❧ 1 ❧

The Law of Abundance Is Natural and God-Given

Concept

Since the beginning of time, philosophers, visionaries, and great spiritual leaders have talked about the natural abundance of our planet. The difference between being aware of our natural abundance and owning a hefty portion of it is one of the main spiritual lessons we come to the earth-plane to learn. It is the art of controlling energy and manifesting your thoughts and ideas.

We live in a 3-D world that reflects back to us the energy, words, feelings, and thoughts we put out. We're not all well versed in the manifestation technique, and it takes us time to learn it. But that in itself is a great blessing.

Imagine a world where everything you thought, felt, or said suddenly appeared in front of you. Sure you could materialize a million dollars on the kitchen table in 30 seconds flat, but each time you had a disquiet or a fear, you would also have a monster standing up against the refrigerator, trying to eat your lunch!

We come into this sluggish 3-D world with the blessing of a special protection. We can have thoughts and feelings that don't *instantly* materialize in front of our eyes, as they do in some of the spiritual dimensions I've experimented in via the out-of-body state. So the fact that you can't just materialize money may seem to be a hindrance, but it's also part of a greater protection that allows you to learn the art of manifestation without getting hurt in the process.

It isn't hard to see the abundance of our planet. You only have to look at the fruit trees in the fall, the lushness of life. We *know* that money is not rare and that abundance is natural. Buckminster Fuller calculated that if all the wealth of the world was divided equally among its citizens, each and every one of us would be a millionaire. It's natural, therefore, for everybody to be abundant—our natural state is "rich." The things that get in our way are feelings of lack, despair, and confusion; and the inability to master the marketplace of life.

More often than not, we get in our own way—by placing in our thinking obstacles, detrimental ideas, and strange resentments that we have to clamber over to get to the honey pot. I'm sure that by the end of this book we will have sorted that out, and you'll remember what you already know—namely, that life is energy, money is energy, and there's plenty of both.

Start by reminding yourself that there's loads and loads of money around. Perhaps it sounds a bit silly, but you ought to begin every day by telling yourself that there is no shortage of money. In fact, there are untold trillions of dollars, yen, pounds, D-marks, and so on swishing about—more than you could ever spend. It's vital to understand that, and to remember that there are millions of millionaires: lovely, rich people to whom you can sell ideas, products, and energy, and so become a millionaire yourself.

We have been programmed by the system to believe that there are shortages and lack, and that uncertainty is normal. It is not. That idea is a psychological racket, designed to control people and keep them in line by making them fearful. Don't buy it. Most people, suffering from a limited mind-set, have no comprehension of just how much money there is actually available to anyone with the will to "step up and collect."

Look at the ancient holy books. You will see that they are full of hope and positive expectancy and abundant affirmations. In the Bible, for example, the words of Jesus are abundant. He lived in abundant times. There is no place in the Bible that says that Jesus wasn't making ends meet, even though Joseph and Mary were supposedly poor at the time of his birth.

However, because we are taught a fear of power, it is naturally assumed that somehow money is evil, that rich people are dishonest and crooked, and that they feed upon little people. While the economic forces of our planet are certainly stacked in favor of the big institutions and governments, there's nothing stopping each one of us from gathering our fair share.

It's hard to align to money if you think it is evil and nasty. But once you come to an understanding that money is neutral, that abundance is natural and spiritual, it's easy to see that having money does not necessarily deprive somebody else. Many of the great teachers have given credence to the idea that abundance is spiritual and that it is your feelings and the power of your thoughts that create abundance for you.

In fact, if you are wealthy, more often than not you will be disposing of your money commercially and charitably, supporting people around you, and adding to the overall velocity and flow of wealth.

As I've said elsewhere in my writings, there are trillions of dollars zipping about electronically on any given day. Those electronic signals are literally passing through your body right now, as are all the TV and radio signals that are in your local area. If you stop and think about the millions flowing through your hands at the moment, imagine making a slight flick of the wrist in order to halt some of that loot in transit, so it sticks in the palm of your hand. A flick of the mind is faster than a flick of the wrist.

Money is good. Greed is not good. However, there is no reason why you can't be very rich, stinking rich, in fact, and still be an extremely spiritual and wonderfully generous person—aligned to the God Force, with a huge heart and compassion for everyone you meet.

Metaphysics

One of the inner concepts we have to grasp early on is that the whole of our reality exists in a wave-particle duality. I'm going to deal with this idea in detail in Law #5, but I'd like to mention it here in passing, as it is a key factor in understanding why some people are rich and others aren't.

What the wave-particle duality means at a quantum level is that our supposedly solid reality is not actually solid at all. Everything exists in an oscillation or a hazy-wave; it is ill defined. This hazy-wave condition remains the same until a particle is observed, whereupon it changes from being somewhere in a hazy-wave state to being solid and existing in a definable place.

The metaphysics of money, and our ideas around money and abundance, follow much the same path as the laws of quantum physics. In order for money to become part of your life, it has to go from a hazy-wave state of ideas—dreaming, wishing, yearning, and vague maybes—into a solid state: a dollar bill, credit in your bank account, a coin in your pocket.

If you can convince yourself at the very deepest level of your being that there is no lack, no unfairness, and no discrimination, and that making money isn't hard, you suddenly open yourself to greater wealth. This is because you've collapsed your self-denial, your aversions, and resentments, and you flip from the insecure hazy-wave state that asks "Where's the rent coming from?" to the solid-particle state. Suddenly you know where it's coming from 'cause the check is in your hand.

In collapsing your hazy-wave money dysfunction, you open yourself to endless points of abundance. This simple click of the mind opens the door metaphysically. Remember, all points of abundance—points in our 3-D reality where money is actually delivered, where transactions take place—are solid-particle states, not hazy-waves.

So to make the manifestation process work for us, we have to put aside all our hazy-wave ideas of lack. We have to become centered and align to the solid symbols of abundance. We have to know we can do it. When thinking about your money flow, say to yourself, *There is a way, and I will definitely find it.* This affirmation works well for almost all of life's little problems.

Action

Take a little time over the next few days to stop and concentrate on things you consider to be manifestations of abundance. Go to places where wealthy people hang out, look at the symbols of their wealth, and affirm that the abundance of this earthly dimension is holy and good. Yes, money can be used for evil purposes, but in itself it has no energy.

In order to make your feelings right, you've got to agree that abundance is natural. You can't look at abundance with anger or envy, and you can't become abundant if you exclude yourself. So when you see a person in a limousine who is wearing fine clothes, if you say, consciously or subconsciously, "What a rat. That lifestyle is not for me; poverty is holy and good," you deny your potential.

It isn't easy for most ordinary people to look at extreme manifestations of wealth and join in the idea. The ego is too racked with jealousy or inadequacy and judgment. We'll look at a palace and say, "That's not my kind of house." We see expensive things and say, "That's far too much for me."

To be abundant is simple, but first you have to be able to join in with your feelings. It's not vital that you can instantly visualize yourself in the presidential suite of a five-star hotel, providing you don't deny yourself the possibility.

In other words, you may say, "I don't have to stay at the Grand Hotel, but it's certainly something I could take in my stride; it's certainly something that I am pleased exists. Moreover, I'm thrilled for the people checking into the presidential suite right now." In this way, you switch from the negative affirmation that money is bad and that poverty is holy to the idea that money is neutral, that abundance is natural and God-given.

So, acknowledging abundance as a daily affirmation is a part of your disciplined action plan. Make a point of noticing the plum tree full of fruit, gaze at fields of wheat, meditate on the endless rows of vegetables at the supermarket, and accept the warmth of the sun as it rises each morning. Also, engage your childlike self, with awe, in the abundance of stars in the night sky.

Each of these are signposts of the Universe-at-Large reminding you that you have the gift of life—that your journey takes place on a planet that is blessed and chock full of everything you're ever going to need.

Say to yourself several times a day, *There's plenty of money in the world, and large chunks of it are just about to drop effortlessly into my lap.* Tell yourself this out loud, for in vocalizing things, you invoke them and make them real. There's nothing wrong with a bit of "fake it till you make it." It's just an affirmation, and anyway, you will make it real in the end. Yes, of course you will!

Money is just a symbol we use to facilitate the gathering of memories and experiences. It assists in interaction with others, and it allows us to come to concepts of honor and integrity, fairness and compassion. It's one way you endorse and love yourself, for it is how you make yourself okay. Using money to nurture yourself is a manifestation of your acceptance of self, your endorsement of self. Can you really love the world if you don't include and love yourself?

Money is in there with you on the spiritual journey; it's a part of the self-realization seminar you signed up for this lifetime. Yet, most are victimized by this idea because they fall for the ego-trap of thinking that their self-worth is linked to glamour, wealth, and their bank balance. You are eternal and worth plenty, even if you are "busted flat in Baton Rouge, and heading for the train...."

And the money seminar you signed up for is just that. A seminar. It has many useful lessons; ponder on them. From money we learn honesty, correctness, and generosity. We also learn the proper use of power; and sometimes we stuff it up, wielding our money darkly, manipulating and terrorizing people, or using our wealth to gain an unfair advantage over others. Sometimes money shows us how covert we are; or worse, it shows us how to be mean and nasty.

Money is a special mirror; it tells us stories about ourselves if we choose to look in it. And from this wonderful symbol, "money," we learn trust and faith and hope. We come to believe in ourselves. We are forced to be creative, look the world in the eye, and offer our energy—our wares. And we are asked to do that honestly and correctly, with kindness for all.

Money forces us to believe in unseen forces, and it helps us to be grateful and to remember God. Money sometimes shows us the road out, when others are dark and sneaky and ugly about the symbol. It shows us many things, money does. It's a friend, harsh and blunt sometimes, but a true friend, nonetheless. We have to believe in money, as we have to believe in our friends, no matter what their weaknesses and faults. Yes, money carries us a part of the way to unconditional love. It does, strange as the idea may seem. So expect the best from your seminar, and expect your friend to show up right away.

Now do this: Get a seven-day candle (one of those votive candles in a glass "jar"), and place it in the southwest corner of your home. With the candle you can place any sacred or power object you may have. Next, you'll write a letter to the Universe-at-Large asking for a cash refund. I'll explain: In this lifetime, you have worked, you have helped people, and you have loved and cared for them. You have generated good energy, much of which you didn't get paid for because, naturally, you didn't expect to get paid for kindness. But you are entitled to a cash return for all that love and energy you put out, but only if you *ask* for it. So ask.

Tell the Universe, *Hey! I've done this and that, and I've worked diligently on myself, and I've helped others. And as money is only energy and I've put out loads and loads of energy, I want a return of that energy—a refund—and I want it in cash and right away. Or, anyway, as soon as possible.* Add a sentence that says you love and believe in yourself, that you love and believe in others, that you know the world is abundant, and that you feel worthy and entitled to your cash refund.

Light the candle and put the letter with it. Then each day, visit your sacred spot and ponder on the imminent arrival of your refund. Do this until your refund appears, restating your affirmations and replacing the candle each week for as long as necessary. It's okay to leave these candles burning all the time—just make sure they're in a safe place.

Expect a surprise. You'll be amazed. When I did this exercise, I waited for a few weeks, then $30,000 dropped in my lap unexpectedly. *Nice refund,* I'm thinking.

❧ 2 ❧

The Law of Flow

Concept

Everyone can get their head around the idea that abundance flows. We watch it daily, flowing and not flowing. Here's the subtle trick to being in the flow.

But first, let me remind you that a positive attitude goes almost without saying. The more you moan and affirm that you don't have enough money, the more it slips from your grasp. Maddening, really, for when it slips away, that in itself becomes a negative affirmation of how unfair the system seems to be. Of course it isn't unfair; it's just energy in motion, responding to feelings. "To those who have, more shall be added," and to those who don't have, a chunk will be taken away.

So the first rule of flow is to constantly tell your mind that you are rich. There are many manifestations of wealth that aren't necessarily cash—love, friendship, nature, sweet sensations, pleasing emotions, etc, etc. "Rich" is a way of viewing life. So tell yourself: *I want to view the world with a kindly eye; I want to view it richly.*

Remember, your unconscious mind, the powerhouse of the soul, doesn't know if you are rich or not. If you tell it you're rich, it will accept that as gospel. So you have to believe in luck and flow and goodness even when, cashwise, things might be bloody awful. Perhaps it goes against the grain, but if you see your affirmations as just that, affirmations, you can affirm your abundance and good fortune even when things look a bit dodgy.

The poorest person has things to be thankful for, so affirming your abundance is an act of gratitude and humility, as well as a way of keeping yourself in the flow.

People get into trouble understanding flow because they can't tell the difference between effort and struggle. So they'll get an idea, and everything tells them it's not working. And yet they plug away, doggedly going through the agony of it all—because someplace, back there somewhere, someone told them that whacking their heads against the wall was an honorable way of conducting themselves.

Not quite so. Struggle causes a lot of pain because it involves a lot of negative emotion. Struggle is also very hard work.

All ideas that are holy and good and honest, ideas that serve humanity and yourself, will have a positive energy of their own. When you head out to materialize a moneymaking plan, it will gather momentum. It's as if the Universe-at-Large leads you step by step, showing you the way. That's flow. You meet the right people, you sit in the right seat on the plane, and next to you is the very person you need to connect with. It's a wonderful thing, watching flow in motion. We all know what it looks like when it's working; the trick is to be able to pull back when things aren't flowing.

As I said in my little book *"Life Was Never Meant to Be a Struggle,"* struggle is effort laced with emotion. As humans, we are required to exert effort in order to get things done. So if you're cycling up a hill delivering loaves of bread, you will expend calories pedaling. Effort is natural. But when one's energy expenditure gets wrapped up in loads of negative emotion, that's when you flip to the unnatural—from effort to struggle. At that point, you should pull back and ask yourself loads of simple questions, questions that highlight silliness.

Of course you need perseverance when times are tough, but perseverance mustn't trip you into negative emotion—that will destroy your dream real quick. So if things aren't flowing, watch the signs very carefully. What little adjustment can you make to get things moving? Is your plan realistic? Do you have the wherewithal to pull it off? Are you missing some component? If you're missing a piece of the jigsaw, what does that piece look like? Is the piece inside you, or where will you get the bit you need?

It's okay to go up a path a little way only to discover it's not right for you, as long as you realize when things aren't working and pull back. The trick is to evaluate and ask yourself: Is this a stupid idea or not? Am I going about it ass-backwards or what? Do I need this suffering, or is my suffering voluntary?

Remember, it's not a defeat to pull back when things aren't right. You can always wait for things to change. The fool plugs away regardless of the signs. If you are aware, you'll pull back, or perhaps continue slowly forward, watching carefully, making adjustments as you go. Remember, don't be impatient; things always take longer to materialize than you think they will. That's because our minds can move faster than the 3-D reality in which we all exist.

Also, it's okay to make mistakes. It's okay to fail sometimes. See these as mini-seminars you attend to teach you the tricks of life. Of course, the main trick is to be flexible and easygoing and lighthearted, and to learn, learn, learn. Life's a seminar. We learn by stuffing it up! So be kind to yourself.

Although flow often seems to be a form of magic, it actually stems initially from order and planning. It's much easier to experience a great good fortune when you are organized and ready and able to receive the abundance due to you. So ask yourself, *Am I ready?* If someone shows up right now with my special opportunity, can I respond? Am I flexible? Can I move and go in an instant? Flow is energy in motion. So you have to become the embodiment of energy in motion—that is, flexible, fluid, and fast on your feet.

In passing, let's look at risk and reward. To make money, you will have to take risks, even if it's just your time on the line. The key to risk-taking is knowledge. For example, gambling is betting on an unknown outcome; investing is betting on known possibilities. The difference is knowledge and the quality of your information.

So, when the amateur blackjack player is pitting his money on the run of the cards, he's gambling. But the professional card player has knowledge and additional information; he can count cards as they come past and make informed decisions about what is about to happen next. He's not gambling; he's investing his money in a planned and reasonable way on what may seem to others as random outcomes. His knowledge and ability change the random nature of the game into one of near certainty. He is not struggling, he's working, just as the croupier and the cocktail waitress are working.

So struggle can be avoided by collecting information—lots of it—learning and watching and topping up on your game of life. Moving through life with ability and knowledge, you go from gambling on life to investing in life.

We all have to accept risk. Crossing the street is a risk, just one we are used to. The trick is to have enough information so you're betting on outcomes that are almost certain. When the outcome isn't certain, you ought to design your involvement to ensure that there is an easy and inexpensive escape route.

Remember, as I've said before elsewhere, never go into anything without figuring out where the exit is. Never commit until you have to, and not until you have enough information. Try to make sure that there is a back door to whatever commitment you make—unless, of course, you are very, very sure of your involvement.

Metaphysics

The metaphysics of flow is easy to comprehend. You figure it with your feelings. Your feelings are enormously powerful; they are your extrasensory perception. The mind can deduce from what it already knows and guess at an outcome. And millions are lost every day using this intellectual guessing method. But your feelings are more accurate, for everything is energy.

So any deal or investment, or any involvement with others, has an energy of its own. That is its thumbprint, if you like. Use your feelings to stay in the flow and to keep away from trouble. Remember, if an idea *feels* wrong, it *is* wrong.

That's not to say you should trash a deal whenever you have a moment of disquiet. It's just to say: If suddenly there is an energy shift and you are in tune with your feelings, that shift will alert your feelings. When something feels odd, stop and notice and take stock. Your feelings guide you away from trouble. Half the trick to making money and being in the flow is staying away from the deals that don't work. It's the deals you walk away from that make you rich, as much as the successful deals.

So put your feelings into everything, meditate, and become a satellite for your subtle feelings. The way to build up your sensitivity is to ask, ask, ask. Constantly refer back to your feelings to confirm your direction. If you are in a meeting, mentally reach out to the other people there, and imagine your arm extending to touch one of them in the heart. Then mentally pull your arm back quickly while centering your mind, blanking it, and ask, *How does this person feel?* Edgy? Arrogant? Angry? Excited? Crooked? Safe? Loving? Kind? and so on. Your first impression will be the correct one.

The litmus test of referring to your feelings should be used many times a day. Energy shifts constantly, so you'll want to be aware, especially when dealing with other people. How does this situation/person feel right now? How is that different from the way it felt last time I checked in? Is this deal I'm considering for real, or has something changed? What's the upside, what is the downside? Is the downside far greater than the upside? Is the risk worth taking? Then ask yourself how you feel. Are you happy, comfortable, and flowing along, or is there something bothering you?

Staying in the flow is really only a matter of staying close to your feelings. Struggle comes from a lack of awareness of self and from poor-quality information. It is also compounded by the inability to turn back when the energy on a particular path peters out. Stay in the pocket, be aware, shift and change, and never get into anything you can't walk away from. Keep these rules, and you will always be in the flow.

Action

The action of flow is one of being alive and aware, ready to step forward fearlessly. You have to move toward your target. So do something each and every day that improves your situation and takes you closer to your dream. Sometimes that action may just be a simple thing that grants you more stability, or more order—like perhaps you take a day out to tidy up your paperwork. Order of itself is a positive thing, is it not?

Rarely do opportunities find you; usually you have to be moving toward them. So heighten your ability to stay in the flow by heading out, talking to people, making contacts, stepping out from where it's safe and cozy, pushing against your comfort zones, and reaching out. That's how the faucet of flow is turned on—by generating energy each day so the Universe-at-Large can engage its magnificent laws and deliver to you even more energy.

Try this: As well as moving toward your goals physically, through action, simultaneously clear a path on an inner level by blowing love and Light out ahead of you. For example, if there is a person in your way, your (female) boss, for example, start every morning by sitting quietly and seeing her in your mind's eye. Bring her up close to you so you are almost eyeball to eyeball; then breathe a long breath in, and expel that breath out into her heart. No matter how antagonistic you may feel, send her Light and love, and do that ceremoniously 11 times. She will change, you'll see.

If you need certain people out of your way, don't wish them harm or evil, just do this: After you've finished the 11 breaths, visualize them very small in the palm of your hand. Look down on them from above; look at them standing there in your hand, an inch high, for example. Then hold your hand up to your mouth and expel a short, sharp breath at them. Literally blow them away, saying, "I release you with love and Light to go in peace to your highest good, but go!"

Using this method, I got rid of a bothersome IRS tax agent who had been harassing me for 18 months. A few days of this metaphysical hurricane, and he quit the service. The next bloke assigned to my case was so overworked and confused and stressed out that he closed my file with no more objections.

If, say, you're off to an important meeting today, breathe in the location if you know it; see it in your mind's eye if you have been there before; or visualize the people. Or, at worst, just imagine the meeting. Breathe in 11 times, and send love and Light to that location. Remember to tell your mind approximately what time the meeting will be. So say, "I am projecting this love and Light to such and such a location for use between the hours of noon and two o'clock or whatever."

Use your inner power equally with your outer strength. That inner power places good energy ahead of you. It gets rid of dodgy people and helps close the gap between you and money. That brings us to the next law of money, which is the law of distance.

—m—

3

The Law of Money and Distance

Concept

In order to be abundant, we have to be close to money. Often our relationship to money follows a push-pull, love-hate pattern similar to our other relationships. Sometimes a marriage or an interpersonal relationship may seem intimate on the surface, but in reality it might be quite distant on an emotional level. It may be that one of the partners is pushing the other away, or that they're *both* pushing each other away—perhaps because they're silently angry at each other.

You have to look at the distance between you and money. Are you close to it and pulling it to you, or are you distanced from it and/or pushing it away? Naturally, the closer you are to money, the more likely you are to receive plenty of it.

The law of distance breaks out into three distinct categories: emotional, intellectual, and physical distance.

Let's talk about emotional distance first. If you have subconsciously established an emotional distance from money over the years, and if that distance is embedded deep in your mind, an anti-money veneer develops around you like a rhino's skin. It's a bubble of energy that disempowers you, denying you access to the green stuff.

In a weird way, the anti-money veneer is trying to protect you from acquiring money. It establishes itself over the years. It's partly due to any anti-money feelings you hold, as discussed previously, but mostly it is sustained by what you feel about yourself.

I'll deal with that in more detail when I talk about money and love in Law #10, but one example is self-hate. If you don't respect yourself, it's hard for people to grant you worth, so people will always undervalue you. If, say, you've always felt yourself to be an outcast, you may exclude yourself from the marketplace of life because you've excluded yourself socially.

So, you may find that you're always just too late for the real money; you just miss the boat because your energy isn't inclusive enough. Not being able to include yourself, you find a subtle way to deny yourself the very thing you want.

Meanwhile, you may still act out the chase, trying for the deal but not quite making it. This way you can feel okay about your efforts. You can kid yourself that you've tried real hard, but deep down you had your inner sabotage program ready to kick in. It's the mind's way of falsely endorsing itself, saying, "I tried hard, so I must be righteous and good; and I only just missed. What bad luck. It's not my fault." You see yourself as an honorable struggler denied through no fault of your own.

Similarly, if you don't feel you are worthy or if, say, toxic shame was imposed upon you at a young age by your family, you may feel bad or worthless. So it may be hard for you to know you are worthy of love and appreciation. And in this case, you'd also have the tendency to give yourself away too cheaply. You become the suffering servant, abused and vilified no matter how sincere you are. It's your shame coming back at you. It's very subtle sometimes; shame is a rotten little critter that tries to eat your sandwiches when you are least aware.

Shamed individuals beg for approval by undervaluing themselves. No matter how good they are and how much they do, they will never feel worthwhile until they heal the shame. If shame is a problem for you, read *Healing the Shame That Binds You* (Health Communications, 1988), by John Bradshaw. It's a wonderful book, and Bradshaw is a cool dude. He'll help you get your head around the problems of toxic shame.

Shame and self-love is another one of those seminars we sign up for. You heal it by accepting yourself. Easier said than done for some, but in the end you have to let go and not resist; you have to control your mind and come to reconciliation. "I am what I am, and what I am has a spark of the God Force in it. And the God Force is all compassion and forgiveness. If I can align with that compassion and forgiveness, I can forgive myself and go past my shame." Which, after all, may not amount to very much anyway.

By the way, make up your mind to forgive others for their transgressions. You can never forgive yourself if you hold on to antagonisms. Past events are history. Today we're writing a new history—a happy tale about how well you did, and how loving and accepting you are of yourself. It's a little book written in the stars called *Cutting Myself Lots of Slack*. A bestseller, I reckon!

Kick the shame and make yourself right, no matter what; otherwise, that pesky critter nibbles on your leg, costing you money all the way. Don't undervalue yourself to win acceptance. Remember, there's no shortage of money, and it's fair and reasonable to charge for your energy and your time; it's the way you endorse yourself.

Obviously you can't go over the top and starting asking ridiculous prices, but you can start upping your price. Paste up a new price list in your mind: Stick 10 or 15 percent on it right now, today. Then put 20 or 30 percent more energy and value into what you do. In a month or two, you can announce the price hike. Then several months later, you can announce another price hike, just as fast as you feel good about yourself. Try to get the energy and value in first, so others don't react too much to the hyperinflation of self-worth your personal economy is undergoing.

To close the distance between you and money, you have to detach from a negative self-image, and you must include yourself in. You have to *join* money and life in your feelings. You have to make yourself right and okay. You must know you are worthy. But, more than that, you must be able to tell others you are worthy—by asking for their money without allowing self-hate and shame to bite ya bum.

Many believe that asking for money is unholy or wrong. Most won't even admit they want the money they aren't asking for. Weird! Our society is preprogrammed to keep us all poor. You don't have to ask for oxygen, and money is a type of oxygen. You can't operate out of "If I don't breathe, will you love me? If I don't charge you, will you consider me holy and good and a nice person? Will you accept me?"

If asking is an issue for you, practice, practice, practice. Start at the bathroom mirror. Imagine your customers, boss, whomever, there in front of you. Imagine them asking you, "How much do I owe you?" And see yourself smiling as you pause to mentally double your price, and listen while you say unashamedly, "$30,000, thank you." See your hand out, waiting to receive your self-worth in the solid-particle form.

Once you realize that the emotional distance between you and money might have occurred because you've acted against yourself in the past—disempowering your chances, establishing a distance between you and money—you can fairly easily *click* your mind and start including yourself.

A good thing to do, as part of your abundance affirmation, is to include yourself in socially. Go to the street party, show up at the dance, attend church, seek people out, and make it a discipline to include yourself. Remember, the more people you know, the easier it is to make money; people are the custodians of the planet's wealth. Knowing people is almost as good as cash in the bank.

If you have created an emotional distance between you and money in the past, take a moment to ponder on what those emotions might be. Write them down and really look at them. See where they came from. Then realize that all you have to do is change your mind, and act out that change by sidling up to where the moolah is.

At the same time, you have to work on how the bubble of anti-money protection built up around you. Some of it is shame, as I said, but most of it is suppressed anger. Once you identify what feelings you have suppressed, you can start owning them.

Once you realize you *are* angry, you can release it. Whack the cushions with a bat. Rant and scream and shout. Release the anger, saying, "I am *angry* because I'm not getting paid as much as I'm really worth." Let it go.

You can change the situation later and raise your prices, but first you must release the emotion. You can't get a pay raise when you're angry. People will react to the negative energy and will resist you. They'll perceive—consciously or subliminally—that you don't love yourself, so why should *they* acknowledge you? They may even try to cut your money because they see that you are devaluing yourself.

Write down on a scrap of paper what it is that irritates or frustrates you, the things that make you angry about money and the way it flows into your life. If you perceive that certain people are blocking your access to money, include them on your list. Try to be honest with yourself. Telling yourself little fibs and being covert with yourself is partly how you established the distance in the first place.

Truth may be uncomfortable in the short term, but it's preferable to the long-term frustration, anger, and struggle that come from a lack of awareness—especially if you have to sustain a lot of half-truths or lies. Say, for example, you tell yourself that you're working hard, but you know that you are mostly doing "busy work" and avoiding the difficult stuff; and that you're loading up on actions that look good but get you nothing. If this is so, you might get very pissed off by your lack of results, without being aware that you are acting as a terrorist against yourself, sabotaging your bottom line.

Once you are honest, you can make adjustments. If, for example, you kid yourself that you are brilliant at what you do—when, in fact, your performance is sloppy and inferior—it limits your ability to get to the truth and really improve. Usually you'll claim that your lack is because of outside forces, luck or whatever. Most people you meet are fairly useless at what they do; you know that because you see it every day. Now this sloppiness of attitude, this laziness and lack of effort, does not necessarily apply to you, but we can all evaluate and improve, can we not?

On the other hand, you might have created an emotional distance between you and money because you have capped what you will give. So you might eke out your energy, limiting what you will provide or do for others while expecting the Universe-at-Large to dollop great quantities of goodness upon you effortlessly. You have to be ready to serve and to give. You don't have to give money away necessarily, especially if you don't have much. But you do have to give of your heart. You have to be emotionally generous and willing and open, not tight-assed and closed.

If you expect the Universe-at-Large to increase your income ten times, it's hard for that to happen if your heart is closed and you are no bigger as a person than you were before. It's simple to comprehend. Big heart=big money. Little heart=little money, and lots of rip-offs, missed opportunities, deals that go sour, etc., etc., ad infinitum. Easy-peasy-lemon-squeezy, anyone can work that out.

So, closing the emotional distance means opening your heart, going past your resistance, stepping up to bat, and including yourself in the process of life. You have to be present and aware. You have to join, not avoid, the issue.

So be open; be ready, willing, limitless; agree to serve. Subjugate your ego for the needs of others, but don't lose your sense of self. Be available, open, and ready, but don't give yourself away either. You can hold on to a strong sense of self-worth and still serve others. It's part of our great lesson in life. It's the act of going from a limited perspective to an infinite one that says money is everywhere, and the more open I am, the greater the potential for me to pull opportunities from everywhere.

Many people resent money because they feel life hasn't been fair to them, that they've worked hard and haven't received as much as they should have—or that they are paid less than other people with inferior qualities to them. However, harboring these negative emotions only widens the gap between yourself and money.

The other concept that fuels this emotional distance is the idea that somebody ought to provide for you; that somehow the world owes you a living. The world does not owe you a living. You have to nurture and provide for yourself. This is the secret to closing the gap between you and money. Rather than blaming others or projecting your disquiet, lack, or anger about money onto other people, begin to own your feelings.

The intellectual distance between us and money usually results from a lack of understanding or knowledge. Sometimes, we just don't know enough about what we are trying to achieve, or we are not well versed in the conditions of the marketplace—the ebb and flow of transactions.

It boggles my mind the way many go into deals without knowing the people concerned, having little information to guide them. Or they accept on face value the information presented without checking to see if it is accurate or not. That's not very clever.

Another important point is that many people never bother to really learn their job or trade. Knowledge is power. The more knowledge, expertise, and connections you have, the easier it is for you to make a profit at the game of your choice.

If you are a commodity trader, for example, and you specialize in pork bellies, you are in a worldwide casino that's betting on the ups and downs of pork-belly prices. You should be up-to-date on what's happening at the piggery; you should be well connected with institutions in the trade and in the flow of information, and you should know how to get hold of information independently and quickly. It's difficult to compete against a casino that is better informed and better financed than you are.

To survive in the commodities market, you need as much expertise as possible and a good dollop of luck. Most people lose. You're up against the pros. And although you might have a hunch and hit a winner from time to time, in the end the odds are stacked against you—unless you know things others don't know. They say that the way to get a small fortune in commodities is to start with a very large fortune. In other words, the market is designed to part you from your money.

Ask yourself, *Do I have enough information about the marketplace, and/or the particular area of creativity I want to be involved in? Am I a long way from the flow of information, an amateur in a professional's world? Or am I ready and up to bat?* Maybe all you need to experience real abundance is to improve your knowledge and close the intellectual distance.

In passing, let me mention another thing that can cause intellectual distance between you and money. There are a lot of money snobs out there: people who believe money is beneath them and that it's not stylish or proper to go for the cash. They are elitists at heart, so they seek to elevate themselves above the concerns of common people by feigning a disregard for the things that concern ordinary folk. Things like earning a living and turning a buck.

Sometimes this elitism is a social-class thing. Sometimes it's a form of spiritual elitism, where a person feels far too holy-moly to be dealing with the trappings of the real world. Don't be a money snob—unless, of course, you've inherited millions—then you can do what you like. The rest of us have to deal with life day to day, and money is a part of taking responsibility and accepting the system.

You might as well enroll for the seminar and get it right quick. That's the most pleasing way; it takes you to harmony and well-being and a stress-free existence via the shortest route.

The matter of physical distance is simple to comprehend. Certain industries are located in certain places in the world. If you're a long way from where the action is, you may want to consider closing the gap. For example, if you want to make it big in movies, you've more or less got to be in New York or LA. It's pointless being in Arkansas if you want to be in films.

Closing the physical distance is a matter of showing up in the marketplace, becoming a face that people know, demonstrating your expertise, and getting into the loop where the movers and shakers are. People who could bestow great opportunities upon you—perhaps hire you or give you a contract—aren't scouring the distant hills for talent. They're in the flow.

The people they know and socialize with are also in the business. And they are communicating with those others who made the effort to show up and declare themselves in the loop.

So, to make it, you have to go beyond your resistance, your shyness or inhibition, and head into the marketplace. It doesn't matter if you're not ready. If, say, you are a composer of pop music and you haven't got all your songs or demos together, you've still got to declare yourself in.

It's a physical, emotional, and intellectual declaration. You have to know what you're doing, be aware of which record companies are buying what acts, who's up and who's down, what's happening and what isn't. It's also a physical declaration of saying, "I'm going to go past my shyness, and I'm going to make the connections and enter the loop, because knowing people is a very big part of closing in on my dream. I'm going to appear and play my songs in clubs, I'm going to put out demos, and I'm going to become a commodity. Sooner or later I will be noticed, and a great prize will descend upon me."

Metaphysics

The metaphysics of distance is connected to the subtle bio-electric energy field (the etheric) that surrounds you. It is a map of your feelings. When you're a long way from money—emotionally, intellectually, or physically—your subtle energy will lean forward toward the few money sources you do have. It will lean against people, begging for opportunities, begging for life to cut you some slack, or begging for a miracle to cover your phone bill. Your subtle energy becomes sloppy because you're leaning away from your power, toward what you perceive as the lifeboat.

When you are solid—when you are taking action, working on yourself—your etheric is strong and powerful. It's not leaning up against life, trying to pillage it. It is standing straight, saying, "I am working on myself, collecting knowledge, processing my feelings, improving my performance. I've brought myself to the marketplace, and I'm at peace with myself. I know money flows; I know fantastic opportunities are available to me. I don't have to lean against people. I can wait, watch, and pick my moment. I'm not whining and begging, globbing on to people like some sort of sticky goop, hoping they'll elevate me or cut me a special deal."

In the metaphysics of distance, you don't lean up against what you want, because in doing so you push it away. Stand straight, nurture yourself, crown yourself king or queen, and work on things that are practical—things that endorse and help you.

Action

It's a simple thing to sit in meditation and differentiate between your intellectual attitude to money and your deep inner feelings. Most people would like to have more of it, but you have to ask yourself if there is a contradiction between what you say you want: "Hey, I want more abundance in my life," and what you actually feel.

Closing the emotional distance is just a matter of deciding, or looking at, what your deep inner-core beliefs are about money—how you will emotionally get off the island of lack, and row yourself over to the mainland where the market is bustling with activity and cash is flowing.

In a moment of quiet time, write down a list of those feelings and attitudes you have about abundance. Be aware of any non-actions that have distanced you from money. Try to discover your core beliefs. Who are you? What would make you happy? What's real and possible and fun, and what's just the ego's disquiet? Delve deep within and ponder; pondering is good medicine. Discovering what you really want saves you endless confusion and wasted energy.

Use your feelings to differentiate between vague yearnings of the ego and your deep, innermost desires and needs. In this way, you will eliminate blocks and highlight any contradictions that may exist.

For example, many would like to be millionaires, but subconsciously they know that making millions often takes a lot of effort, and with that comes a lot of stress. So, intellectually, they would like millions, but their inner truth is different. In effect, their subconscious protects them from something that sounds good to the ego but would actually be a living nightmare.

Looking at the distance between you and money teaches you things. Perhaps all you really need is a bit more money and a bit more security. Now, it may seem an odd thing to say, but you can't get security by earning money. Earning money involves activity, and all activity burns energy, so eventually that energy burn-out makes you insecure. Low energy=fear; high energy=security.

The only way you can increase security is to nurture your-self. All insecurity comes from the fear of collapse: the collapse of a situation, of your life, a business, whatever. So if you need more security, work on your body, be kind to yourself, sleep more, rest, hang out in nature, and do nice things for yourself. No amount of money in the world can make you secure. Of course you *can* combine hard work with self-care, but you have to work at it.

I was having dinner with Deepak Chopra recently. He's a successful author and lecturer, constantly jetting around the world. Yet he maintains balance by finding time to work out no matter where he is and by maintaining a very healthy diet. He told me that every three months he takes five days off on his own. He goes somewhere remote, like a desert, and stays there in silence—no phones, no people, nothing but him and silence. It's a brilliant idea. He rebuilds his energy by pulling back, and then he's ready to zip around for another three months.

Get in touch with who you are. See which motivations are real and which ones come from just the intellect and ego. Per-haps you don't really need the aggravation of piles and piles of activity and responsibility. Perhaps all you need is a carefree life with some good creativity, loads of friends, and plenty of fun and games.

In the end, you must both take care of the inner spiritual self and satisfy the many needs of the outer self. It's a balanc-ing act—like everything is a balancing act.

If you look within and discover that making piles of money is your thing, but you worry about the contradiction that may exist within you, don't despair. It's easy to change the subconscious. You just tell it you have decided to change. You can easily rewrite your subconscious mind; you just keep telling it something different.

You may have to do so over a period of days and weeks, but it's simple to agree to change your mind. It's also easy to see that abundance comes from closing all of the gaps. That idea of itself gives one a lot of hope and determination for the future.

And, of course, it's not just the emotional, intellectual, and physical gaps between you and money. The real gap is always between what you think you want and what you actually want, deep down. Once you arrive at the truth, deep within, you've come home spiritually. You have returned to the source, where your divinity exists.

In there, you will find the truth, the meaning of life. And you will see what it is you want to do, what you want to offer to the world in this lifetime. It's there in the deepest recesses that you find your connection to all things. From that stems a sense of immortality, and from that comes security. Bingo!

Meanwhile, you probably could use more cash, so, as a part of your action plan, do this: Get your checkbook out and write yourself a nice fat check, payable to you and postdated. Then pin it up on your fridge or bulletin board and look at it from time to time.

A friend of mine who opened a shop wrote herself a check for ten million Australian dollars and postdated it five years. Her shops did well and she probably had a few million when a company proposed that she franchise her stores. The deal was worth about seven million. The franchise deal came in with just a few days of the five years left.

In the end, she decided she was into creativity—not into accountants and lawyers and all the stress that comes with a deal like that—so she didn't follow though. She was satisfied, though, because the Universe did provide for her check to be made good, even though she didn't take the potential seven million on offer, which would have given her a total of ten million. I'm sure she'll get her ten million in the end. She'll just go about it in a less stressful way, a way that suits her creativity.

—ⱳ—

The Spiritual Law of Supply and Demand

Concept

Money is important because it is a symbol of your mastery and comprehension of life's great journey. You don't have to become rich, but you do have to have your money trips under control. Commercially, the law of supply and demand states that if there is more demand than supply, prices go up, and if there is an oversupply and less demand, prices go down. But there are other aspects to supply and demand that are less traditional.

To make money, you have to deliver your energy in some form, to satisfy a demand that is out there. And if what you are selling is energy, charisma, and enthusiasm, there is no competition because most others are selling things that are lifeless, loveless, and dull.

So your stuff—your service, your creativity, whatever—will always be different, unique, and desirable. Why? Because you will imbue it with energy, the God Force, love, and caring.

It will excite people and bring them to life. It will carry within it the energy of the part of you that joined, the aspect of

you that celebrates life, laughs, and is carefree—the part of you
that honors humanity. It may just be a garden chair you are selling, but your garden chair will radiate Light and love. It will be
so lovely you could place it at the head of the Round Table, and
no one would think it odd, as your chair is a beacon of Light.
Energy is easy to sell. Everyone is into it. It helps them feel
special, looked after, and secure.

Once you imbue your life, your products, and so on, with
energy, you will see that the law of supply and demand no
longer applies. It only relates to the tick-tock world we see
around us. It does not apply once you understand the trick of
projecting energy into your moneymaking activities.

To properly comprehend the idea, you first have to make a
subtle ego-shift in your mind. You have to switch from focusing on yourself—"What do I need? Who will supply my
demands? What will I eat? Who will give me the things I
want?"—to concentrating instead on the needs of others.

This doesn't mean you have to become a charity worker, or
disempower yourself financially. It's more a way of saying that
your needs will be met once you can find a way of projecting
energy and fulfilling someone else's need. That is self-empowerment. Hoping someone will fix it for you is disempowering,
because a satisfactory outcome always lies beyond your control, subject to the whims of others.

So switch your focus to: "How will I fulfill somebody
else's needs today, and get paid in the process?" There is no
way of making money on this planet other than by fulfilling
people's needs. It's just an ego-shift. First, you concentrate on
serving others, and in that way you serve yourself.

There are more than five billion people on this planet, and every day of the week each one needs, say, a hundred different things. There are trillions of demands that need satisfying. So, rather than looking at supply and demand from a position of insecurity and lack, you can see it from the other side of the coin. There's a perpetual oversupply of demand, and if you can't give people one thing imbued with an energy that shines like crazy, you can sure as hell find something else they'll want. When you are selling energy, you are selling Light, so your possibilities are infinite.

What will you supply? The things humans buy come in three categories: They buy services, knowledge, or products— nothing else. You can raise your energy, you can change your consciousness, and you can align to the divine abundance in all life. But when people are attracted to what you are, you have to have a knowledge, a service, or a product to sell them. Simple, really.

By concentrating on what people need, you become abundant. When we look at the marketplace of life, isn't it true that so many products don't work? How many restaurants have you eaten in that are not clean or customer oriented? How many businesses exist just to screw people rather than to love them and satisfy their needs? There are so many shoddy products and rip-off merchants who haven't clicked into "How will I fulfill my customers' needs?" Often a customer's need may just be an emotional need to talk to you about their life while you're selling them something.

However, in order to get this supply-and-demand thing down right, you have to think in terms of energy and you have to be clear about what you will sell people. Providing a service is not usually as profitable as selling knowledge or a product because, more often than not, services have to be delivered personally. And there's a limit to how many hours a day you can deliver the service, and what price you can charge.

Knowledge, on the other hand, is valuable and easily packaged. We live in an information age; there are hundreds of ways of packaging knowledge. What you deliver in the form of knowledge does not have to be way out, it just has to be presented concisely, inexpensively perhaps, and with originality. If you have knowledge that people want, you can quickly become wealthy.

If selling products is what appeals to you, think of products you believe in, products that are worth the money. Ask yourself, *Can I put my heart and soul into the product? Can I be enthusiastic and really love this gizmo, really serve my customers?*

You have to remember that concentrating on people is a form of love. When you stand in the showroom explaining the benefits of the refrigerator you're selling, it's an act of love—providing you're not coming from the angle of, "I'm selling this refrigerator to rip this person off." It's only love if you are genuine and if you truly concentrate on your clients. By concentrating on them, you are loving them and making them solid. You are offering them a moment of immortality.

So the game is to provide people with something they need, imparting helpful information and exuding a loving energy as you make the sale. You have to join humanity at the level of emotions, needs, and desires. You have to nurture them and be there for people. You have to empathize and put out energy.

If you are there for people on a human level, it helps you sell products. It's love in action. Love in action is a form of compassion. Wouldn't it be great if you could sell a million refrigerators and rack up a whole heap of compassion at the same time? Now that would be a lovely memory to look back on at the end of your life, would it not?

So, to sell things successfully, you have to subjugate your ego long enough to take people's money. This might sound a bit brutal, but in fact it is a religious, spiritual idea. You subjugate your needs—your life, your aches and pains, your experiences—and listen to others. Watch their eyes, notice their body movements; relate to them, ask them questions, and work out "What does this person want?" Then fulfill that want.

Think about how you can improve what you do. Even if you work for someone else right now, start by putting more energy in. If the place you work in is dull and lifeless, put energy in anyway, for by doing that you will catapult yourself out of there to something better.

If you are self-employed, think about how you can make 20 improvements to your knowledge, service, or product. In the end, you are selling yourself. So you'll want that looking good. You need to offer love, kindness, and charisma. You'll want to be big-hearted and right there, bushy-tailed and up to bat. So ask yourself, *Am I eyeball to eyeball with life, ready to serve?* Or does some aspect of your personal agenda get in the way? If it does, put it to one side quickly; put it aside long enough to cash the check anyway. You can always visit your therapist after work.

So, offer beauty in an ugly world; offer kindness where ego and greed predominate; be accommodating and free-flowing when others are uptight, edgy, and stiff. It is so easy to understand. Take the product you are selling, and visualize the divine Light shining upon you. Breathe that Light into your being, and breathe it out, placing the Light into the thing you are selling. If you are a massage therapist, project Light into your table and your little bottles of oil. Most of all, project Light into your hands—before each session, and, of course, during each session.

If you sell things on shelves, touch them regularly, move them about, make them come alive, give them energy. The little tins will be refreshed even if they have been on the shelf for weeks and weeks. The more you touch and love the product, the more energy it has, and the more likely that it will belong to someone else in ten minutes' time.

If you sell information, make it original, clear, concise, and idiot-proof so anyone can understand it. How often have you read instructions on how to access some information, on the Internet, for example, and you wonder if it's written in Hindustani or ancient Sanskrit or what. Why is that? Because the person who wrote it was thinking of himself, not you (just say it's a man this time). He lives in his own world, in a basement, with an IQ of 180. He hasn't seen daylight for many years, and the only human he ever talks to is the pizza delivery man. He couldn't care less if you know your www.com or not.

You have to think of others. There are loads of people out there who aren't very clever, but they have money. Will they understand what you're offering? Then again, there are others who are fairly bright, but they can't unscrew a little nut, as their expertise lies elsewhere. When I see the words *easy assembly* on a product, I immediately flee to the safety of the parking lot. I know that if they say it's easy, I'm going to have to hire a rocket scientist to figure it out.

So, what will you sell, and how will you make it irresistibly beautiful? By forcing yourself to supply knowledge, a beautiful service, or a product by imbuing it with gentleness, love, and Light, you are disciplining yourself to go from ego to spirit, from greed to abundance, and from negative emotions to love.

When you concentrate on people and you provide things for them, you are falling in love with them. Choose love to make your life abundant. And that love should be more or less unconditional—as best as you can manage anyway. Never forget that.

Metaphysics

Inside your life energy, personality, and mind is an oscillating molecule of infinite goodness, the divine Light; the Christ consciousness. If you align to that infinity within you, you will always have energy. There is no limit to the amount of God Force you can have.

By concentrating on goodness, processing your shadow side, disciplining yourself beyond bad habits, and meditating on the Light, you will become a Light Being. As you glow effortlessly with this energy, you will project that Light into what you do. So you may not only be selling apples that are nutritious and tasty to eat, but apples that come with a little bit of your God-Force energy.

You never have to compete once you infuse yourself and what you do with Light, so your apples will outsell everybody else's. It's a matter of calling the Light into your life. Put energy in: Visualize Light going into the service you provide; put Light into your CD, musical tape, or the book you are packaging your knowledge in—feel the manuscript bathed in Light. Or feel your product to be part of the God Force, albeit a tiny manifestation of such goodness.

Remember that you are a teacher, you are helping people, making them feel safer, taking them from fear to love, from ignorance to knowledge. You are hauling them with a bag of apples from restriction to freedom. By mentally pushing these ideas into what you do, you are projecting the Light out from yourself, and you are offering God. People will buy a Godlike apple a long time before they'll buy an ordinary apple.

Once you have the God Force in what you do, there is no more competition, and you are no longer a victim of the vagaries of the market, the ups and downs of supply and demand. You're out on your own, miles ahead of the rest.

I know a young man who opened a shop. It was minute, just two little rooms; the whole thing wasn't much bigger than the average kitchen. The shop sold candles, incense, aromatherapies, and so forth. Heaps of other places in the town did the same thing, but he was a bit different so he wasn't in competition with the others.

The young man was soft and kind and loving. People would come in, and he'd be right there for them. He'd talk to them, make them feel better, and they'd go out of his shop with a bottle of ylang-ylang extract or something. I'm sure many didn't know the difference between ylang-ylang and ding-a-ling, but it didn't matter—because it felt safe and correct and nurturing.

He had a little fountain in the doorway and that felt nice; and the shop was spotless. The few shelves he had were always fully stocked and neat; little signs explained things, and he explained things; and you could pop in for a remedy for your granny's arthritis. He couldn't fix it necessarily, but you'd wind up with a candle or a book or something that was imbued with tons and tons of love. That would cheer your granny up, her immune system would kick in a bit stronger, and she'd get a bit better.

He sold love 12 hours a day, 6 days a week. He was humble and kind and soft-spoken; and if he had an ego, it certainly wasn't around during working hours. People loved him; they flocked to his shop.

After several years of selling love in little packages, he sold the shop for over $500,000—an astounding price for a few hundred square feet of shop. He used the cash to make another investment and did the same love-love thing there. Now, eight years later, he's worth three or four million, and his company will soon go public. When it does, he'll receive an enormous refund—with a note from the God Force saying, "Here's 20 million bucks, dude. Thanks for dishing out all that love and sweetness in a dull gray world."

Action

Get a piece of paper, and write down the services, knowledge, or products you are familiar with—the things you're already doing. Then write another list of things you might be interested in delivering to people.

Having honed down your lists, look at your products, services, and packaged information, then analyze what other people have done in these fields. Ask yourself, *Is this other product exciting? Does it challenge? Does it inform? Does it teach people something? Does it enthuse them and make their lives more comfortable? Does it help them to be sexier or more beautiful? What is in this product that has value, and how could it be improved?*

Perhaps you could take a very ordinary product that everybody is familiar with and add a little something that makes it absolutely irresistible.

Look at your commercial life so far. What have you sold? Let's say you've always sold your labor, and you're working for somebody at present. What can you do to put more energy into the labor you provide? You might say, "I get paid the same amount of money whether I put more energy in or not," but this is not the point.

If you energize yourself in your work, you will find that: (1) the job becomes more fun to do, (2) you'll be more likely to be promoted or given a raise, and (3) you'll lift your energy so high that you'll go beyond the job, and hop perhaps to another corporation that pays you twice as much. And you do this by arriving a little earlier, staying a little later, improving your efficiency, and making an effort to relate emotionally to the people around you.

It is good to practice putting energy in right now, no matter how dull the current situation. Later in life, that energy will become cash in the bank or abundance or wonderfulness of one kind or another.

Under the metaphysical law of supply and demand, you should not limit how much you're going to put out. You don't have to let the world use you, but you have to give because you want to receive. So start by giving. Give of your attention and concentration, give of your love, and give of your energy.

Don't destroy yourself with negative feelings toward other people; if you can't love them, be neutral. Be enthusiastic, be open, and be up there for it, for in limiting yourself, you get stuck in one place in one salary for the rest of your life.

As you agree to *give* as part of your action plan, and as you begin to look at how you can improve your service, knowledge, or product, it will take you to the next step. It carries you to a higher energy, a greater velocity, a larger salary, and bigger opportunities. It opens you to easy money. You'll find some money, or win some, or a great dollop of moolah suddenly will drop into your lap. Expect a payoff!

—⟋⟍—

❧ 5 ❧

The Law of Money, Concentration, and the Wave-Particle Duality

Concept

I touched on wave-particle duality in Law #1 as a key factor in why some are rich and some aren't. The wave-particle duality of the subatomic world shows us subtle qualities to the getting of money that we've only recently begun to understand.

What we learn from quantum physics is that all subatomic particles exist in two states. Initially they are in an amorphous, hazy, ill-defined wave-state; meaning they are not solid. Once we decide to observe a particle, the act of observation collapses the hazy-wave, and suddenly the particle becomes solid—with a real identity and a defined location. That's how our 3-D reality becomes solid. You do this strange magic trick every moment of your life: You make life real by observing it.

Our brain and consciousness is a quantum field like any other. You are trillions and squillions of little particles. Your mind and your consciousness are signals given off by a subatomic field of energy. Our money-gathering activities seem to follow the same quantum law. Money and financial abundance exist in both a potential hazy-wave state and an actual solid state. The solid state is easy to comprehend: It is the cash and credit you use every day. When money is not in its solid-particle state, it exists only in its hazy-wave state—as a check that may arrive, a possible lottery win, a deal that may happen, and so on.

The act of taking money out of its "maybe" hazy state is the act of manifestation. That act is accomplished by observation. At any given moment, there are trillions of hazy-state dollars that potentially could become yours. And it's through the power of your mind and the power of concentration (observation), that you collapse money from a distant hazy-wave maybe to solid wealth, cash in hand.

Concentration is how we pull to us the opportunities we need. Yet we have been taught that concentrating on money is evil, or at best a rather undesirable trait—a bit greedy and egotistical. In Europe, children are taught that wanting to make money is close to satanic.

If you went to a group of European university students and said, "All I want in life is money. I am concentrating on learning about it, and money is my goal. I wanna be rich," they'd look at you like you'd come from another planet and had leprosy. Yet these very same people are happy to live perpetually on government handouts; that is considered normal. Anyone working or creating things is weird. It's amazing how the ego will flip black to white and back again.

There is nothing wrong with making money, providing you do it without hurting others. And it's vital to focus on money;

it's the only way you can become abundant. When you fall in love, you devote time and energy to that one person, and a bond develops between you. When you stop concentrating on them, the romance fades and you fall out of love. Same with money.

Do this: Take a note out of your pocket and stare at it close up and notice every detail. Keep your eye on the note for 15 minutes without looking away. Say to yourself from time to time, *I'm concentrating on money, it's my new discipline.*

Yet there's a big difference between concentrating on abundance—taking concerted action in the marketplace, developing your skills—and greed. Greed is the capturing of more money than you actually need, and accumulating it to the detriment of others.

You have a divine right to abundance, and if you are anything less than a millionaire, you haven't had your fair share. Even if you *are* a millionaire, there's nothing to stop you from acquiring more money. You can then use it to assist others and spread goodness and Light.

A friend of mine worked out how high a stack of £10,000 worth of 50-pound notes came to. Then he cut little pieces of paper and made up stacks, putting a real 50-pound note on top of each stack. In this way, he placed a hypothetical million pounds on his kitchen table, and he concentrated on them. He was an office cleaner, but 18 months later he has his million and several million more. Get a pair of scissors.

Falling in love with wealth is hard for most people because they don't see concentration as a form of love. And maybe they don't trust their own motivation. But you can have lots of money and not fall into the egotistic trap of power and possessions. You might want the money to fund creativity and help others, you might want it for mobility or acquiring knowledge, or you might just want it so you and your mates can play and have fun, be lighthearted and worry-free. There are many just and humble reasons for concentrating on money.

Each moment, your potential shifts via the quantum field of your mind. Some of those biomechanical quantum shifts take you to less money, poverty, and struggle. Others take you toward more money, abundance, and wealth.

The first thing to do is concentrate on the abundance you *do* have. Make it solid and real by acknowledging it. It's easy to overlook the many things we are granted—oxygen, the blood rushing through our veins, the food we eat; the people we know, the love we have for our friends and family, the companionship of animals and nature; the warmth of the sun; the sustenance of water, the air, and the earth. All these things are around us; they're our "temple," so to speak. We have to be grateful for what we have.

The concept of the wave-particle duality is the understanding that you will act in one of two ways. In affirming that what you have is abundant, you collapse all the negative possibilities of lack. On the other hand, by being emotional and fearful and focusing on what you *don't* have—focusing on the problem rather than the solution—you intensify the confusion. You empower the lack, and your chance of collapsing the hazywave into its solid state becomes less and less possible.

Which takes us right back to: "... whosoever hath, to him shall be given..." The Bible writers were talking subatomic physics when they wrote that.

Metaphysics

The metaphysics of the wave-particle duality are slightly more complex. It lies inside the subtle bioelectric energy that exudes from your body. This energy, often referred to as your subtle body or etheric, is where your feelings exist.

As I said before, you are a feeling. And that feeling, or thumbprint of what you are, is inside the etheric. So part of transforming the way you handle your life—not just from the point of view of abundance, but your personal power as well—involves developing a solidity inside that bioelectric/etheric field.

This consolidation of power can come about in many different ways. One of the fastest ways to raise your energy is to be more disciplined—to take time out to exercise, eat well, meditate, and pray—take time to develop order. And time to establish a positive expectancy, to see your life flowing. All these things will raise your energy, but, more than anything else, you have to begin to oscillate at a higher level.

Oscillating at a higher level is opening yourself up to the Light and the abundance of the God Force that is in all things. So, enter a meditative state, and feel the Light moving through your subtle body. Keep your meditation simple. See the Light coming into your heart chakra, into your throat, and then on up into the center of your forehead. Feel the Light streaming down through the crown at the top of your head.

Know that Light is everything, that you are everything, and that you are the Light. You can, therefore, be everywhere. But once the concept of "I am Light" is firmly established in your mind, you exit the finite world of the ego/personality and enter the infinite world of your spirit. Now you are enormous, everywhere, eternal.

Now feel the whole of this planet *inside* your heart. Visualize planet Earth as a small entity that is orbiting your heart, around and around. In this way, what you are saying is, "I am bigger than life. I am bigger than my circumstances. I am divine Light, eternal, so I am metaphysically larger than the confined space of this planet or my life's day-to-day needs."

It's a matter of standing astride the whole planet, like a huge colossus with the earth at your feet, knowing that you are in control of your life—and that there's a magic and a power all around you that will bring you endless rewards. We don't have to understand the mechanism of how it works; all we have to do is know that it *does* work. Deepak Chopra says in his book *The Seven Spiritual Laws of Success* (Amber-Allen Publishers, 1995), "Inherent in every intention and desire is the mechanics for its fulfillment...intention and desire in the field of pure potentiality have infinite organizing power. And when we introduce an intention in the fertile ground of pure potentiality, we put this infinite organizing power to work for us."

The trick, therefore, is to keep your energy pure so your potential remains fertile. If life is swamping you emotionally, if you feel timid and unsure, the subtle energy you project doesn't go forward. In fact, it collapses back on itself—which is why in troubled times, people often say, "My God, I feel like everything's collapsing around my ears." This is the sensation of your subtle etheric closing in and coming back to protect itself because it feels weak, much like a small animal who huddles in a corner when a predator attacks.

Express your energy outwards. You don't have to be perfect to be confident. Know that you are the Light, and know that you can move your energy to any distance across the earth-plane. You can touch people and pull opportunities from tens of thousands of miles away. Distance is not involved when you live at the level of the divine Light of God's abundance.

There is no distance, so there is no limit to how far you can reach or how well you can do. The infinite nature of energy has within it the mechanics for fulfilling your dreams. That's certain. We watch it happening every day.

Action

As part of concentrating on money, you will need to take some money action. Money doesn't move of its own accord. If you drop a $100 bill on the street, there it stays until somebody picks it up or the wind blows it. Similarly, abundance involves you moving toward opportunities.

It's in the act of motion that you generate energy, and, as I said previously, money and energy are the same. So each day, take one defined, concerted action that will assist you in your money-gathering activities. Plan out the deal. Print the brochure. Attend the conference, whatever it takes. Action, action, action. Lots of it. Meanwhile, continue to do things that help strengthen your feelings. As I said in one of my books, you can go to the most expensive hotel in town and just sit in the lobby and have coffee, but you have to move toward the thing you desire.

You have to join in your feelings so that the abundant world, which you are entitled to be a part of, is not something strange to you. So it's not hazy, unobtainable, or laced with negative energy. As you move toward abundance—walking in and out of expensive shops, having a coffee in the Grand Hotel—buy the financial papers, if you don't already get them. Most stock exchanges have a visitors' program, so go visit the exchange even if stocks bore you silly. Join, join, join.

Become comfortable with the idea that you and abundance are not separate and different. You are money, and it is you. Gone is the hazy-wave; now comes the solid particle you manifest through concentration.

You have to think in terms of the potential for abundance as a natural part of your energy, your subtle body. As you take action, it's like water going from steam to ice.

Action is a manifestation of power. You have to have power in order to collect money from people, so it's vital that you now reinforce your affirmation of abundance by taking action. Taking action doesn't have to cost you anything. You can walk in a field of wheat and notice how much wheat there is, or you can walk down an expensive shopping street saying, "Wow, these clothes are really beautiful. When the time is right, I will acquire as many of these as I want. Aren't they lovely?"

Take actions, any little action, for it's not necessarily one particular action that gets you the money. They all act as affirmations that you will help yourself. The real money may come from somewhere else.

Via action, opportunities go from possibilities to probabilities and into reality. Then you can haul them around to the bank, "clunk" them onto the counter, and say, "Hey, this used to be a hazy-wave, now it's a check-style solid particle. Please be so good as to credit it to my account. Thanks."

—⟋⟍—

The Law of Invocation and Manifestation

Concept

First there was the Word. Sound is a major force in the act of creation and manifestation. It's another part of the mysterious mechanism that moves our thoughts and ideas from the hazy-wave state to solid reality. We have to invoke our desires, call out to the Universe. We must tell it what we want, not just think about what we want.

When we speak out loud, verbalizing our reality, we engage the manifestation process. Sound is a part of that which creates our individual reality. Each moment of our life, we either invoke or destroy our dream. We call upon it to become a fact, or we cancel our previous instructions.

When the shamans of old called for rain and suddenly it pissed down buckets, everyone thought it was great magic. But people didn't understand how the process works. In fact, it was only the power of invocation, with a bit of help from the shamans' connection to the nature spirits.

Invocation is like dealing with a mail-order company. You call the clerk on the 800 line and invoke your order, "Send me this. Send me that..." So, begin to state your needs out loud as fact. For example, you might be having coffee with a friend and you say, "A great financial prize is about to descend upon me." They might ask, "How is that?" And you answer, "I am invoking what I know to be true. I know it is true because just by invoking it and believing it to be true, I transfer my idea from a hypothetical, potential universe/reality to this 3-D reality. As I invoke, I create what I need."

A couple of months ago, I started doing this very same invocation, and a little while later a stock-exchange friend suggested I invest in a small mining company he knew about. I bought about $75,000 worth of its shares, and within 30 days I'd cleared several-hundred-thousand dollars profit. There's something very fine about invocation.

After that success, I started a new invocation. It said, "A big and important opportunity will come to me in the next few months." One morning I wrote a short treatment for a movie. It was a simple idea, expressed on a couple of pages of scrap paper, and written a bit amateurishly. I'm not a film writer, and I know nothing about movie production or scripts. A few weeks later, a friend of mine introduced me to a very nice film man, and I gave him the treatment. He loved the idea.

What I didn't know about the movie business is that you need a fleet of ten-ton trucks to haul people's egos around, so nothing is easy. Anyway, I soon found out that making films is no fun at all. In the end, I decided it might be best to quit the movie business while the quittin' was still cheap.

You have to be careful when you invoke, as you are going to end up getting what you ask for, and maybe what you ask for isn't any fun. Now maybe I'll make movies one day and maybe I won't—it's irrelevant. What is cool, though, is watching the invocation process working.

So now I'm thinking, *This is the time of my life that I should find a permanent partner, settle down, and make my life more steady.* I've traveled constantly for 20 years. Now I need a place I can call my own, a settled existence. So my invocation says, "Either my present mate and partner will marry me in the next six months, or I will meet the lady of my dreams and she'll consider me the fella of her dreams. And the whole settling down/family issue will be fixed before next Christmas, tickety-boo." Sorted! I'll keep you posted on how things go.

So decide what you want and invoke it. Don't waffle or daydream; don't voice any maybes, uncertainty, or doubt. The Universe-at-Large can't get its infinite head around wishy-washy doubt. Either something is, or it isn't. Be firm. Be certain. Be absolutely definite. Don't say, "When I get this, and if I get that, then and only then will I experience my dream." Instead, invoke your dream as fact.

Remember, in the realm of the infinity of energy, there is no time; everything is eternally present. So all your dreams are a reality right now in some parallel universe. By invoking your dream as a given fact, you haul it from a parallel place to right here, right now—in your warm, clammy hand, to love and behold and enjoy. *Coolissimo!!!*

Metaphysics

The metaphysics of invocation are hard to comprehend and explain. I can't absolutely say why it works or what the real technology behind the law is. It seems to me that, as we give voice to our reality, we not only move the air, but we also move the etheric reality around. Just as our bodies have a subtle bio-electric reality (etheric), the whole planet and the ambiance around us has its own etheric body. That body may very well be connected to other parallel universes, wherein our hypothetical ideas and dreams exist.

When we invoke, we seem to haul those ideas from hypothetical, possible universes to this one right here on Mother Earth. The important thing is to believe in what you are invoking, and don't voice any deprecating ideas. Keep your dream safe; guard its holy and sacrosanct nature by not trashing it with negative waves.

Don't engage in idle chatter and thoughtless remarks. If you say, "This situation is a nightmare," you invoke terrible spirits to visit you at night. If you say it's dreadful, you establish fear and dread in your life. If you say something is a pain in the butt. . .be prepared for a hemorrhoid attack. Don't moan, and don't allow doubt and disquiet to diminish your life and its power.

If you are worried about something, keep it to yourself and don't vocalize it as fact, for that solidifies it. Work instead on the solution. Voice that solution as fact. Everything can be changed. Catherine Ponder says in her book *The Dynamic Laws of Prosperity* (Devorss & Co., 1988): "Never underestimate the power of words. You make your world with words, as did Jehovah in the beginning. But if you do not like the world you have previously made with words of discord, lack, limitation, and hard times, you can begin building a new world of limitless good and prosperity by changing your words of command and decree."

So there you have it—invoke the Word, and get the abundance and happiness you are entitled to.

Action

Prayer is a form of invocation, especially when we pray out loud. But to make prayer really work for you, you have to make the subtle shift from asking and begging to knowing. If you say "God send me more money," that's not an invocation; it has an air of uncertainty about it. It feels weak. Invocation requires you to state your need as granted, and to be certain that your loot is already on its way—delivered and real in a parallel universe, and on its way to this 3-D reality we call home.

So instead of praying quietly, pray out loud, stating each desire as fact. Remember, "A great prize is about to come into my life." "A very profitable opportunity is on its way to me." "A large sum is dropping into my lap effortlessly," and so on.

Invoke, invoke, you'll never be broke.

—ɯ—

7

The Law of Money and Ego

Concept

The function of the ego, among other things, is to concentrate on keeping you alive and to give you an identity. The ego wants to separate you from others, so it is naturally competitive. It believes in and promotes exclusion rather than inclusion. The ego needs specialness, distance, and separation from others to feel okay and to go beyond its fears and insecurities.

The number-one ego-driven force fueling the planet, other than sex, is money. Money is a symbol of importance, and feeling important allows the ego to believe itself distant from other people. When there is distance, the physical body of the person in which the ego dwells can be observed. As I said in Law #5, at a subatomic level our reality exists in a hazy state. It's nowhere and everywhere. It's only when you observe something that it becomes solid, so the ego likes to establish observers.

I explained in *Whispering Winds of Change* how, in order for you to observe something, you must be distanced from it. So distance, elitism, and specialness play to the ego's tune. This is why ordinary people adore the famous and like to associate with them. Because celebrities have so many observers, they seem to exist in a well-defined particle state and thus give the illusion that they are more solid and secure than ordinary folk.

They seem very real and larger than life, not in the usual hazy-wave state of other strangers. So they are seen by the millions as special glitzy particles. This helps ordinary people feel that their own energy is higher and safer—because they have bumped into a *celeb' a famoso* of extreme particle wonderfulness.

It's all a bit silly; it's an illusion. Celebs are not more secure than you are; usually they are very insecure and neurotic—the ones I've met anyway. And, of course, no one can permanently pick up your energy; you have to raise it yourself. Anyway, there is no high or low, is there? But the idea of importance and specialness excites people, and it sells newspapers and advertising, but it is not real, is it?

The trick is not to fall for all this specialness routine. It's an ego trip, and it burns loads of energy. Trying to convince people that you are okay, or trying to get them to admire you and see you as special, wastes time. In the end, it will cost you money. Once you establish such a view with others, you're a big shot and you have to pay for dinner!

You can buy fancy cars and spend loads of your hard-earned loot sustaining a theater. That gets you the odd ego-boost, but it doesn't get you permanent happiness, serenity, and harmony. And it doesn't take you to the Oneness in all things. In effect, it carries you away from your spirituality and from God toward the illusion. If things go wrong, your ego will take it all personally, and you'll become sad and morose.

That's why people take money so seriously—not because it keeps them housed, fed, and comfortable, but because of their need for attention and specialness. Once you detach yourself from the ego's need for attention—once you've worked on yourself, and granted yourself worth regardless of how imperfect you think you are—then you don't need admirers and observers. You become a self-observing individual, a free individual, out from under the manipulation of the ego and the world of glamour-addiction that dominates so many these days.

As you become free from these impositions, you begin to detach from the life-and-death struggle the ego goes through. Suddenly your relationship to money changes. You are no longer scared and holding on to every cent with a vicelike grip. You relax, for you see how money is often just a game the ego sucks you into for its own ends.

It's one of the ways the ego controls you, keeping you edgy and stiff and in prison, brainwashed into accepting its ideas. It's difficult for most to understand how that stiffness and fear causes them to miss opportunities. Unravel the baggage, shift your mind about the need for importance and specialness, and suddenly you are free. After all, what you really need is a happy, liberated, creative life. Seeking admirers and observers is for the weak and insecure; you are not a performing dog, acting out, hoping for attention and a tasty morsel. It's degrading and debilitating, and spiritually it's rather ugly.

There is no greater abundance than the abundance freedom offers. To unshackle from the ego's manipulation of you is to transcend. It's a hairbreadth from total enlightenment. What is the point of being enormously wealthy if you're neurotic and scared? What's the point of being famous if it means you create for yourself a luxury prison of sadness and loneliness? Surrounded by yes-men and minions, but without the company of real friends who love you, who accept you unconditionally—people you can love in return.

As I said in *The Trick to Money Is Having Some*, "Moneymaking is not a serious business. It is a game that you play. At first it may seem that it is a game you play with the forces *outside* of yourself—the economies of the marketplace, so to speak—but as you proceed, you discover that it is actually a game you play *with* yourself." Detaching from the seriousness of money involves moving from ego-oriented ideas to a spiritual comprehension of money.

Once you are no longer separate from the rest of the world and you have joined the Infinite Self within, you are back in the divine Light that connects us all. You see the evolution of the earth-plane as a combined evolution of all the souls upon it. So rather than grabbing and pulling to make your assets and valuables separate from everybody else's, you realize that you are a part of everything, and everything is a part of you—which means, of course, that everybody's money and wealth becomes *your* money and wealth.

This helps you enormously, because it opens you up to the possibility of receiving large amounts of other people's money without having to actually do any work: like winning a lottery, finding money in the street, coming upon a fantastic moneymaking opportunity, or whatever. Poverty is established by the separation the ego creates; it's the root of poverty consciousness, if you like. By becoming a part of all things, you create an abundance consciousness.

Seriousness is a disease of the ego. Life isn't really serious; it's just a short journey. Yes, there may be pain, anguish, and other negative emotions in your life, but those negative emotions are generated by contradictions of the ego. The ego wants life to go one way, and then circumstances come along and contradict it. Our journey on this earth-plane, when viewed in its spiritual context, is a completely positive experience.

Seriousness warps your life and disconnects you from your childlike self. The creative power inside you is childlike, and creativity equals money. If you deny yourself access to the child within because you're too serious, you also block your connection to the divine Light and your feminine self. Every creator who's any good uses their feminine side to create with—whether a scientist working on a hunch, a painter working on the interplay of colors, or a musician dealing with the juxtaposition of notes and chords.

The feminine principles are soft, and they appeal to human feeling. In fact, creativity is the only evidence left of our societies once they've come and gone. We don't remember the businessmen of Rome or the various generals that fought the Trojan wars. Even the kings and queens of old are fairly uninteresting. What we value is the art, the architecture, and the feelings of bygone societies. What they believed in, what they did, the art they left behind—the Colosseum, Versailles, paintings, books—those are the things that have meaning, and so they last. We remember the yin, because it is through the yin and softness that the God Force is expressed.

So if you are a little too serious, lighten up, dude. Try to make light of life; embrace its childlike beauty. Being too grown up is a serious and painful experience. Don't mess with it too much.

Metaphysics

The metaphysics of money and ego are simple to understand. You are an oscillation of energy; a feeling. If "having and not having" money is linked to your ego's perception of itself and your overall perception of your self-worth, your emotions will be on a roller coaster, and that will affect your subtle body. When things go wrong—the check bounces, money's not flowing—your energy will drop. You'll feel defeated, weaker, and less than before. If you are locked into the ego's perception of life and things go wrong, it can make you unwell.

Somehow you have to come to the metaphysical truth of your divine specialness. This is not a specialness that you poke in people's faces, but a silent specialness. It's the act of accepting the infinite beauty within you. Then the ups and downs of money are irrelevant. To get to that point of view is not an overnight process for many, because everything we ever hear tells us how important status is, and how lacking we are.

All advertising is there to remind you of what you haven't got. Its function is to stimulate the desire by subtly showing you an inadequacy. Often advertising uses subliminal fear mechanisms. You don't want to be fat, do you? (And therefore rejected by others.) So buy these special foods. You don't want wrinkles, do you? (And therefore be lonely and unloved.) Rub this useless cream on your face. You want admirers, don't you? Buy this glitzy car that will fall apart in two years.

Advertising also stimulates debt. Debt is a form of leaning. A bit of debt, manageable debt, is okay; lots of debt topples you over. It takes you into fear and negative emotion, which affects your etheric energy. Once the etheric starts to wobble, you have less protection from outside forces and psychic intrusion, and you may experience even more fear, get depressed, and so forth.

The way the government and the media play to the ego is an insidious control trip. It's designed to make you a prisoner. The only defense you have against tick-tock's bombardment of you is to detach.

By detaching from the need for observers, and decoupling the idea of money as a status symbol, you disempower the ego—which allows you freedom. You can just be you and free. Yes, you can have aspirations, dreams, and desires, but they shouldn't be obsessive. You have to live life in the meantime, and you have to have fun. If you are not having fun, something is very wrong.

Look upon money as the driving force of your creativity. See it as solidified love, and don't use it as a security device. Then your emotions will be stable, and you'll be liberated and stress-free. Use your money to buy fun and lightheartedness.

Action

As I said in the Concept section, lightening up and becoming less serious is the key to changing money from an ego-symbol to what it actually is: a symbol of the appreciation of energy. It's part of becoming less and less complicated.

Most people are tied up in knots; their life takes endless management and sorting out. Take action. Toss out stuff, gently and kindly get rid of the people you don't need, and sell assets that are a drain on you. Manage your time better, and get rid of all your superfluous commitments.

Stay in the pocket, and keep it all as simple as possible, given your circumstances. This way you'll come to the childlike self. When you find that inner child, parent it, nurture it, and look after it. That action of itself will grant you all the security you will ever need.

You can never reconcile your life unless you rediscover that inner child and learn to keep it happy. Go to a toy store and buy yourself some games, play in the rain, roll in the mud, or whack your face into a cream pie.

I was once in a la-de-da restaurant in San Francisco with my ex-wife, my little boy, some kids, and a bunch of other relatives and friends. It was a very expensive restaurant—extremes of la-de-da—with lots of very serious, important people dining in whispers, having dull dinners. At the end of the meal, I ordered a whole bunch of gooey meringue pies. It wasn't on the menu, so the chef had to make them up especially for us. The maître d' ceremoniously brought the pies out and placed one in front of each of us; we were ten at the table.

We waited for a second or two, staring at the pies with glee. Then on the count of three, each of us at the table picked up our pie and whacked it in the face of the person sitting to our left. We all gave, and we all received! The children went ballistic, laughing their heads off. We fell to the floor in hysterics. We couldn't contain ourselves. The maître d' was shocked; there was sticky meringue everywhere. Some of the other customers were laughing fit to burst. Others were absolutely appalled, and they've probably never gone back to the restaurant again. The sugar in the meringue stings your eyes a bit, but boy did we have fun!

If you've never done something like this, try it. Being light-hearted is angelic, and being angelic is being infinite. And being infinite is easier than being stuck with a bunch of boring grown-ups who fret over their investments, and who strut and work hard to pay out money for stuff that doesn't make them happy.

If you are suffering from negative emotions or pain, internal-ize it and work on it on your own. Do not project it onto others. You have to be responsible and own your own pain. Sure you can talk about it to a therapist, or you can share your troubles with a friend, but in the end you are your pain. It's personal to you. You don't have a right to project it onto others, leaking anger and dis-quiet, spoiling their energy by dolloping your stuff upon them. That's bad karma, as is manipulation, vengeance, and nastiness.

As part of setting you free and liberating yourself from fear, don't bother to push and shove and compete with others. If they need to be hot shots, let them. If they need to prove how clever they are, let them. Act simple, and just listen. It's a good disci-pline. If they need to be first, step aside, let them pass. The sun will rise at exactly the same time for everyone in the neighbor-hood—no matter who rushes ahead or who ambles along at peace with him- or herself.

It's the belief that you have to compete that creates lack, and the fear of lack. Once you raise your energy, you don't need to compete. And once you don't need to compete, you're no longer scared. When you are no longer scared, you resonate a stronger energy, more people show up, and you can bill 'em all the more. These laws of money are so simple!

—〰—

❧ 8 ❧

The Law of Giving and Receiving

Concept

People get confused about giving and receiving because they wonder how much they should give in order to receive. Sometimes they wonder if they are receiving a fair share. But the concept is easy once you look at it from the point of view of emotion, and not money or chattel.

The way to ensure that you will always have enough is to forget about the money and concentrate instead on giving of yourself emotionally—that is, supporting people, putting out energy, and being there for others. People are scared and insecure, and they need emotional support; they need protection. It costs nothing to give it to them. To do so, you have to put aside your problems and worries; you have to subjugate your ego, get underneath people psychologically, and push them up from below.

You practice listening, empathizing, really hearing what they are saying—instead of cocking an ear politely in their direction while thinking about something else. Look them in the eye when they speak, repeat back to them words they have used so they know you have listened and understood them. When they are negative, come up with a few words of consolation. Recognize that their emotions are painful for them to bare. Say, for example, "Gee, I understand, that must be tough; it must be very disappointing for you that such-and-such a thing happened."

Don't buy their emotion; just be there for them while they let it out. Don't try to fix things. People usually don't need fixes; they just need a strong, kindly person to listen and to empathize. A few "there, there's" is all it takes.

Show interest in life and humanity and people. When you meet people, ask them questions: Where were you born...Who are you...Are you married...Where do you live? Be there for them, and listen, listen, listen to the answers. Concentrating on people is loving them, so agree to concentrate. That is emotional giving. It helps people feel more secure.

Then, never deprecate them or their efforts. At best, you might suggest, in a nonthreatening way, some other course of action—one that might be stronger, more likely to succeed than the course they've embarked on. Never trash people or dump on them. Never say things that might hurt them or scare them. Always try to keep them safe.

Make these laws of giving a part of your code of living. You will fail as we all do, and you'll get annoyed and lose it, but keep trying. For, in the end, you have to fall in love with life and yourself; and falling in love with humanity is one of the ways you learn to love yourself. It's the first hurdle in the giving game.

It's the way we master giving, and in doing so we develop a spiritual quality; we develop charm. Through it you become spiritually prettier. People respond to that. They will seek you out. Emotional support and protection is kind and benevolent. In a harsh dog-eat-dog world, it's pure heaven when you meet someone who's benevolent and kind and there for you.

Once you have the emotional giving sorted, the rest of it follows along naturally. You give of money and gifts depending on what you can afford. You don't have to spend a lot. Sometimes a small gift, well chosen with the recipient in mind, is more valuable than something that costs a lot.

When I was in the jeans business years and years ago, there was a chap who came into the warehouse regularly. He had a company known as The Good Fairy. Whenever he visited, he arrived with a small present. It was often just a few sticky buns or chocolate or cold drinks, something like that. Everyone liked him, and we cut him all sorts of special deals on the jeans he bought.

He would have had his sticky-bun money back from us a thousandfold in discounts on jeans because he thought of us and took time out to stop at the bakery before he came in to do business. He had giving and receiving sorted out. He was a very humble kind of guy, and he made millions in jeans and the property business. Good luck to him, I say.

So the giving and receiving trick is not to be self-centered, and don't be a scaredy-cat tight-ass. Remember: There is no shortage; money is energy and you are energy and there is plenty of both.

So give emotionally to others, and open yourself up to being there for others; be kind and emotionally generous, and never rob people of their positiveness or their hopes. Always build them up; never deprecate them, even if you consider their ideas a bit silly. Back them verbally and emotionally, without condition. And, if you really can't bring yourself to back them unconditionally, then at least be neutral, as I said.

Now to the receiving. Get your head around the idea that everybody's money is your money. Do things that allow you to truly comprehend that the world is yours. Go to the art gallery in the town, look at the great works, and place the image of those pictures inside your heart. They are yours. Go to the jewelry store, and mentally place those fine things inside you as well. It's nothing more than reaching out in your mind's eye for a necklace, pulling it back, and placing it inside you. It's now yours, rather than being unobtainable behind the window as you gaze at it from the street. Look at the fine things of life, and own them mentally; let them belong to you.

Now let's start to affirm these ideas as true. Go take a thousand dollars out of the bank, and try to never walk around with less than, say, 500 bucks, even if it's the last of your money. If you can't manage a permanent float of 500 right now, then settle for less, but carry cash with you everywhere you go. Of course if you can manage more, carry a couple of grand. Don't worry about losing it, or those negative waves about being robbed. You are in flow and balanced and in charge of your money—no one's taking it from you—in fact, they are lining up to give you more.

Get used to having money in your pocket, knowing that you are abundant and that more is coming, and knowing that you are responsible and you won't go potty and blow it all in ten minutes if you can't afford to. Carry real money, not plastic. Credit cards have negative connotations; they are often a symbol of lack, not abundance. They are a mechanism that appeals to the ego, and so they control people.

Using credit cards, people overspend, and that trips them into worry and fear, for the bill is on its way. Don't use credit cards unless you have to establish credibility, like at car rental companies. The rest of the time, use cash. It's solid and real, and it helps you feel rich. Its presence in your pocket is an affirmation that you have money and that you are open and ready to receive even more.

Next, believe in your abundance. When bills come in, pay them the same day. If you don't have the money yet, because, for example, you are waiting for payday, write out the check today anyway, and postdate it or leave the date blank. Put the checks you owe on your desk, nice and neat in their envelopes, waiting in line to be mailed. Don't allow bills to rob your spirit of its hopefulness.

Be prepared to pay cash for everything right now and on the spot. After all, you want to receive right now, don't you? So don't contradict that by hanging on to money that's owed to others. Cut the check, and know that the universe will provide.

Quickie: If you are massively in debt and out of control, file for bankruptcy. Get rid of all the old money aggravations, and tell your creditors and the Universe that you are sorry for mismanaging your life and for denying people their rightful payment. Then, never accept credit again.

I went to America an illegal immigrant with very little cash. It didn't take me long to rack up a whole load of debt. That obligation and the weight of the emotion it caused me, slowed me down a whole bunch. One day I decided to sell everything and pay off large chunks of my debt, even though it would leave me with no assets in hand. I decided to pay all new bills in cash on the day they arrived or—because I traveled a lot—within a few days of my getting back from a road trip.

Then I did a deal with the people to whom I was in debt, and they agreed to monthly payments. My biggest creditor was a sweet man named Bob. I owed him $55,000, so I sent him 55 thousand-dollar checks. Every month, his money went through, and eventually I didn't owe Bob a dime; he got it all back.

I made the affirmation that I wasn't going to live in the emotion of lack anymore, and that even though I didn't have enough to pay all my old debts, I was ready to reform and simplify my life by creating no new debts. In addition, I agreed with myself to work especially hard to settle my old obligations. Doing this changed my financial situation around. It took me several years to get it all sorted out, as I was originally almost $400,000 in debt. But in the space of five years, I settled everything, including paying an ex-wife $100,000; and in addition to paying my debts, I made and saved several million dollars.

Make the affirmation that you are abundant enough and disciplined enough to go to a cash basis, paying for things as you go. Soon your whole outlook changes. You go from desperately needing to win a little time for your bills, to being serene and at one with your money trips. Suddenly, this mind-shift clicks into the Universe-at-Large, onto your side, as you are now coming from strength.

That solidity pulls money to you more and more. Of course, first you must go past your resistance to letting go. It's weird how it all works. I reckon it's your fearlessness and self-discipline that effects the change.

I should also remind you that, as part of your affirmation that you are open and worthy to receive, you will have to practice accepting what is offered to you in life. I deal with this idea a lot in my other books, so I won't dwell on it here, but let me remind you of the rule.

First, whatever gifts you are offered, no matter how useless or grim the gift might be, take it. Never refuse to receive. Worst case, you can always give that dreadful vase to someone you don't like!

Second, never refuse money from anywhere. If friends offer to pay for dinner, let them. Be gracious and thank them and tell the Universe, "Thank you for paying for my dinner." If a person wants to pay you for some inconsequential act, accept. And never ever walk past money on the street without picking it up, even if it is just a small coin. Humble yourself, and stoop for it.

It doesn't matter what others think. You can't put out the message that you are too proud or too uptight to receive free money. The Universe doesn't know the difference between a dime and a million. If you refuse the dime, the Universe thinks you don't want money, so you collapse your chances. Accept all that is offered to you, even the mucky coins in the mud. Make it a rule never to refuse anything that comes to you for free.

Metaphysics

The metaphysics of giving are silent and center around the projection of your etheric subtle body. When you express hope and cheerfulness, when you are expressing outwardly, emitting energy, your etheric is like the sun. Remember, I said that negative energy makes your etheric collapse in on itself. The more you get used to projecting outwards, the longer your etheric reach becomes. It's an inner reach.

So give silently. When you pass people on the street, mentally reach out and touch them in the heart and silently project the thought "love," or project admiration for them even though you don't know them. Back them, believe in them; project goodness, hope, and positivity. If you see that they are upset, project the word-thought "serenity" or "calm." If you see that they are angry, project "peace." Don't judge them; know they have some inner issue unresolved, probably from a long time ago. Love them even if they appear a bit ugly.

Make it a rule never to pass a person in the street without projecting some kind of silent goodwill. Now, if you are coming out of the Tokyo underground in the rush hour and there are 60,000 people there, don't mess with trying to get them all. Pick a few here and there, and leave it at that—otherwise, energywise, you'll be on your knees. But keep projecting silently for the eventual healing of everyone on the planet, silently touching people you pass, without them knowing—like the way angels touch us in our sleep without us being aware of their presence.

That's the metaphysical giving sorted out. Let the receiving come in from the inner worlds. For as you displace energy out from yourself into our external 3-D world in a positive, silent way, you automatically pull more from elsewhere in the inner worlds. It comes to you as you project out, and it also comes to you in the night while you sleep.

The energy coming in is pure spiritual Light, and so you will feel more energetic, or you'll have more stamina. Sometimes the Light comes to you containing information. A thought goes off in your head, and suddenly you realize your need to buy $100,000 worth of aluminum futures, and so you act on that intuition and you buy them. Eventually, everyone else decides intellectually that aluminum is a good thing, and the price goes up. And you got the inside tip weeks ago; you've cleared your position, you're at the beach projecting the word *relax* to the vacationers who pass by, healing them bit by bit, one at a time.

In a world where almost everyone projects uncertainty—some make a living projecting fear, and governments have whole ministries devoted to sustaining fear—it's a cool little whiz that knows how to turn his or her energy the other way, and give out security. It makes you different—silently different. The energy builds over time, I promise.

Action

One of the best actions you can perform in relation to giving and receiving is to keep a gratitude book. I understand that Oprah Winfrey recently picked up on this idea, and she's been talking about it on TV. (Also, take a look at the book *Gratitude: A Way of Life*, by Louise L. Hay and Friends [Hay House, 1997]). I haven't seen Oprah's show, but here's the technique in case you don't know it.

You keep a journal of all the things you are grateful for. You write in it every day as a discipline—Oprah suggests five things each day. It's a way of pulling abundance to you. In the act of being grateful, you are acknowledging your abundance. The fact that you have to take, say, five minutes to write in your journal each day means that you are observing your blessings, so you make them more real. Your mind projects more satisfaction and less lack, and so more good things come to you.

—⁕—

The Law of Honor, Integrity, and Abundance

Concept

Talking about honor is tricky. It doesn't take much to come off as a righteous *Pratimus Maximus* of extreme pomposity and silliness. Here goes. I'll do my best, and I'll keep it short.

When you separate from your body and look back at life, nothing will have disappeared. I've been in those worlds via the trance state, the out-of-body experience (OBE), and the Near-Death Tube, and what I tell you is correct, although each one experiences their "life's overview" slightly differently. You won't want to look at stuff if it's gruesome. If your life has been one of manipulation—inflicting terror, nastiness, rip-offs, and so forth, the moment of your spiritual overview is going to be an extremely painful experience—unless, of course, you change things now.

You can metaphysically and spiritually rewrite your history by seeing your mistakes as lessons, understanding that the God Force is full of compassion, and realizing that each of us falls into the dark through our weaknesses and fears. In addition, the people who have been affected by any darkness you projected had a metaphysical responsibility. They must have projected or sustained their own negative energy for you to show up, or at least they must have had options and they didn't take them.

Of course, in the case of children who are abused, they don't have options because they are born into negative situations.

If darkness has been a part of your life, you can perform a spiritual overview and healing while alive. First, you have to ponder your dark side and agree to let it come out, as it is usually repressed deep within. Then, when you are ready, take yourself off for a couple of days on your own—someplace remote and quiet. Stay in silence and fast, meditate, and pray.

Allow the impact of your acts to come upon you, and, once you have looked at that, all you have to do is own it. That is, you will have to see how you were responsible. Owning it is accepting that you inflicted the pain on others, and you have to see how it must have felt for them as they became scared or sad because of your actions. Perhaps you killed them off because they lost hope, or perhaps they died not because you killed them literally, but because you stressed them out so much that they passed away from other maladies.

You use your two- or three-day quiet period to look at your dark side, to process and acknowledge your hatred and antagonism. You agree to come to an act of contrition and to atone.

Contrition and atonement sound serious and Biblical. One imagines balls of fire cast down from above, while Sodom and Gomorrah burn in the distance. It's not quite like that, because a universal compassion kicks in if you do it right. Contrition is feeling sorry for your stuff-ups and owing them, and atonement is doing something about them.

We all have darkness inside us, so you don't have to feel especially guilty. Yet you can't get to the Light without passing through the dark. The idea that you can escape it completely by just being positive is metaphysically unsophisticated. You can certainly avoid it for a bit, building Light and energy as you go, but in the end, it is always there, and you have to tackle it one day. Rudolph Steiner called it the Guardian of the Threshold. I always imagined the guardian as a monster on your path who knew all your weaknesses and could play on them—it would eat you if you didn't have the courage to face it.

Even the most saintly people have a dark side. If they say they don't, they are saintly people with quite a lot of BS and denial, and that of itself can be dark. Even Jesus had his 40 days in the desert processing his shadow side, being tempted and so forth.

As your energy grows and grows and you become more and more Light, you have to come to honor and integrity, for the expanding Light within you attracts the dark forces that hang around looking for weaknesses, looking for ways to use, to their own ends, the power you are creating. Now people usually believe they have no dark side or that they have already processed it, but that is not often the case. Most have simply repressed their dark side deep within, so it's not obvious.

Simultaneously with this process, you will want to be 100 percent correct in your future dealings with people. So all your future financial dealings must be honorable. You have to be completely fair and honest and 100 percent correct with people.

Next, you have to have honor in your feelings. That means living in the truth and expressing that truth and not being covert. We are trained as children to use covert ways to get what we want, and so we don't see it as dishonest. But it is. Our world is very dishonest, and our leaders encourage dishonesty by setting bad examples—by lying, being corrupt, and using political sleight of hand to sustain power.

People come to believe that being dishonest, covert, sneaky, and manipulative is normal. It is not; it's very dark. Being on a power trip is also dark. That power may come from your physical strength, or it might be a financial, political, or military power. Sometimes we become experts at wielding sexual and emotional clout, tormenting others with our control over them.

Almost all power is abused. That's how we learn. We have to become strong inwardly and outwardly, without misusing the power we have. It's very hard to get it right, and most of us err. Some lust for power. They get off on emotionally or psychically capturing others and maneuvering them. Bad karma.

We are also taught to lie, exaggerate, and obscure fact. We lie by omission, seeking to sustain one image while living another. To the student on the path, all of these are traps, and they have to be sorted out, for when you lie, it is to yourself. When you cheat, it's the same. When you manipulate, you are creating a prison for yourself as well as your victims. In the end, everything you do is to yourself. There is only the Oneness, so all acts are self-infliction.

Metaphysics

The metaphysics of honor are simple. You can't hide from the truth. So you have to let go, humble yourself, look at the truth, and fix the bits that are less than best. Each of us has fear, hatred, and antagonism; each has cheated emotionally, financially, or sexually. We each have our transgressions. You rewrite your history by looking at that. Perhaps it may result in your suffering a "dark night of the soul," but it will pass as you grant yourself forgiveness. Gradually, the power of the infinity within you bathes you in a new light, and you are made whole. In this way, you complete your act of contrition.

Action

Atonement is the act of making good. So you go back and you pay off, if you can, the people you cheated; you apologize if you have hurt people; or you atone by charitable acts and good works. Perhaps you can't repay those you owe, so you make a donation to some cause from which they might benefit.

Atonement is accepting full responsibility for what you have done without too many explanations and excuses, and realizing that you hurt people because you were trained that way as a child, or perhaps you allowed your fears and weaknesses to lead you astray.

Then you vow that you will act lovingly and kindly to others for the rest of your life. You follow through consistently over a period of time, making good the hurt you have inflicted.

I don't think it's enough to just feel sorry and say you're sorry. Sometimes you have to do something concrete as well.

You can make all the money in the world and you can buy all the experience possible and live a rich life, but a life without honor and integrity is completely worthless. So as part of your abundance affirmation, and the setting up of a new energy in your life, include the correctness of honor if you have not already done so. Live your life impeccably—on every front—financial, emotional, and sexual. And if you exercise power, be benevolent, very benevolent.

—ɷ—

❧ 10 ❧

The Law of Love, Compassion, and Money

Concept

Most people can't get their head around the idea of money—love and compassion being linked together. The idea that money can be a symbol of love seems odd—we are so programmed the other way. Here's how they are linked; it will help you see it all in a different light.

There's a psychological war that goes on in us humans between self-hate and self-love. It's a part of another battle that persists: the energy war between living and dying, building energy and depleting energy. The two issues are wrapped up with abundance and love, and they can very dramatically affect your ability to earn money and pull abundance to you.

Here's the concept: You start prebirth as an infinite spirit in a spiritual dimension. There, the spiritual memory of what you are is eternal, and so you have existed in some form or another since the beginning of time. Suddenly, the spirit energy that is the real you finds itself inside a little body, trapped there for life, collecting new experiences.

The act of coming into the body is one of descending, leaving the magnificence of a domain of spiritual Light and entering into solidity and restriction. Physical restriction and emotional difficulties; perhaps the restriction of a dysfunctional family; poverty, disability, whatever.

It's a sacred and humbling act to accept such a learning experience. It's an act of love, for the restriction will force a consolidation of energy. It will force that spiritual energy to go from hazy-wave to a solid-particle body, and it will have to take on psychological impediments that will help it learn what it is like to be a human.

Those impedimenta are not real to your spirit-identity. They are borrowed from others who have lived before, they are part of the global mind-set at the time of your birth, and so they are imposed upon the spirit. They really don't belong. The spiritual infinity within can't be shamed, dysfunctional, unwell, hurt, or injured, for it is a spark of the Christ consciousness.

People often wonder why a God that is all love and compassion can allow pain and suffering. But it's easy to see that the spirit—the one you actually are—doesn't "do" any pain and suffering. It remains always in a state of grace, a state of complete positiveness—even if it is collecting painful memories that the ego experiences.

By the time a child becomes a mature being, it has downloaded the negative waves of its culture and the global mind— the collective mind, if you like. Your job, then, is to work your way out of that and return to the real you, that spark of the Christ consciousness within. That's the seminar—transmuting the negative into compassion and love. In other words, you are busy re-creating your spiritual identity here in our slowish-particle 3-D world.

We start with shame. Early in our childhood, we are shamed when people shout at us, get angry, admonish us for not using the potty correctly, whatever. Later, we are shamed intellectually as being stupid; or our actions and decisions are invalidated. Then, perhaps sexual shame kicks in as we discover that we are not pleasing to other humans as a sexual partner, or we are very pleasing and are used by others. Sometimes sexual abuse is forced upon us in childhood. It's all very difficult stuff, this little seminar called life.

Psychological shame kicks in as we deal with the peer pressure of our teenage years. You have to be like this to be cool. And if you aren't following the herd, you are ostracized. We are shamed into conformity, even if the conformity is one of hooliganism and drugs. There is conformity in rebellion and the counterculture, as there is in tick-tock.

Now we're doing serious amounts of confusion and pain, and we probably hate ourselves. We want to be something else. At times in our dreams, we remember that we are eternal spirits, but it's a distant memory. Right now we are humans who are insecure and hate ourselves, and we're in various degrees of pain and anguish.

On top of all this, there is the other issue, that of living and dying—high energy and low energy. We have to fight our way out of these fears and restrictions and return to our spiritual identity. It dwells in a dimension of love. So we have to come to love. First, it's a love of self—not a narcissistic egotistical love of self—but more a physical, emotional, psychological, and spiritual respect for self. Can we love ourselves in spite of all we have been told, all the personal defeats we have suffered, the shape of our face, our lack of ability, or whatever? That's the journey.

Initially, the answer is usually no. Self-hate kicks in. We anesthetize the pain via drugs, sex, and illusions of power. Or we use overwork and alcohol to blot it all out, succumbing to our addictions. We feel that if only things were different—if only we had more money, if only we had a different set of conditions, or if only a certain person acted in a certain way—then we would be happy; people would love us, and things would be just fine.

That's the story of most people's lives. Self-hate gets in the way of everything, including their moneymaking ability, because eventually they lose the will to fight on. There's a fine balance to the acquisition of money. It usually involves activity, and that activity takes you further and further from your real self. It burns energy and makes you *less* secure, not *more* secure.

The security you seek is within. It comes from seeing your-self as beautiful, and it comes from going through the healing we talked about in the last section. It's the act of self-love—the acceptance, detachment, and forgiveness of self. It's where you wake up and remember that you are not the spotty-faced teenag-er who was ridiculed and shunned; you are a powerful, eternal spirit, imbued with the Christ consciousness, and here with a mis-sion to fulfill and lessons to learn—a spirit of infinite honor and integrity that has a connection to all the knowledge that exists.

Nobody out there is perfect. We're not trying to compete in the perfection stakes. You can love yourself and be imperfect, as God loves us unconditionally. I really like the image of the water rat, this scruffy little rat that sniffles around on the edge of muddy river banks. It doesn't look like much, but the little rat is sitting there on a log by the side of the river, and he is what he is. He isn't apologizing for being a water rat, but simply stands inside a divinity and a spirituality that is the animal spirit of "water rat."

You are what you are. You might be an Adonis in the making, or an incredible goddess energy, or you might just be a little water rat who stands in front of the bathroom mirror in the mornings and says, "I'm a water rat and that's okay. I don't have to convince people or act to please them. I don't have to work to win their affection. I don't have to pay for them so they will love me, because I love myself. I am what I am. I'm going to go out today, I'm going to believe in myself, I'm going to be honorable. I'm going to concentrate on people and treat them fairly. I'm going to treat myself fairly, for by nurturing myself, my energy will build and I will become secure. I know that money flows *to* security, and away *from* insecurity. So by being more secure, I will prosper."

When you are insecure, it turns people off. To spend money, people have to give away a part of their security. When they make the transfer of money to you, they have to feel solid; they have to feel they are getting something that will make them more, because they are paying out and becoming less right now. If you are solid and contained and secure, it helps them feel solid, so they transfer their cash more readily.

That is why self-hate destroys your moneymaking abilities—partly, as I said, because it's hard for you to include yourself; and partly because you trigger insecurity in others and that forces them to hang on and become tight.

By booming out life force, love, strength, and encouraging words that support people, you express a compassion for people's insecurity. In the process, you become stronger and more abundant. You become a divine paramedic, offering people the oxygen mask of life force, dolloping out goodness and strength so they become less fearful. People will respond to that life force, and it's up to you to figure out how you're going to bill 'em.

Money is a symbol of that life force, of its appreciation. Money can be a solidified form of love. Through the transfer of money, we facilitate love and communication with other humans. It offers us a simple system of providing for and loving and nurturing ourselves, and it is one way of expressing generosity and kindness for the less fortunate.

Metaphysics

The energy war is a simple one to understand. We generate energy and we burn it. Modern life and its psychic and chemical pollution threatens us daily. The personality is perpetually slightly off-balance, slightly scared. We are constantly pushed from love toward fear, so we look for the life force to sustain us. As we fret and worry, we burn more etheric energy and become more edgy.

We imagine that making a pile of cash will help us, so we rush out to seek our fortunes. Often we use work to avoid our fears. When we are very busy, we don't have to look deep within ourselves. But soon our lives are real complicated, and it takes loads of our vitality and ego power to keep things flowing. Our energy drops, and we become victims of our own self-hate. We become lost in the false ego-self, rather than resting in the Infinite real self. Gradually we become numb, existing in a vapid and lonely state.

It's scary, so we look for someone whose energy we can feed upon to sustain us. But once we start trying to suck energy from others, they're not going to like it. They will respond by fleeing as fast as their chubby little legs will carry them.

So as you process your love of self, and as you work on your security by nurturing yourself, you become more neutral, less and less an energy vampire. Eventually you have surplus energy to dish out, and that is how you will develop compassion and true caring for the world and the animals and humans upon it.

Now tell me that money is not involved. Of course it is, for in the getting and dispensing of money, you learn the fine balance of manifestation that I spoke of in Law #1. Through work, money, and commercial activity, you see how there is an energy trade-off between activity and security, and yet another trade-off between love and fear. Then there is the money lesson in the balance of giving and receiving; and the further fine balance between respect for self, self-worth, and respect for others.

How you make money to buy the experiences you need in this lifetime—and how you handle the abundance that comes in—will be very much a part of the final spiritual picture you present when your eternal Self returns to its Infinite Homeland, carrying back the memory of what you were in this lifetime. Money, compassion, energy, heart, love, fear, wealth, generosity, meanness—they are all characters on the same great spiritual stage. The trick is to align to the beautiful ones, step away from the ugliness, and accept the gift of your Infinite Self in the process.

Action

The action of compassion and money is the act of becoming comfortable with life's situations and the state of your bank balance. You have to be kind to yourself, and you have to keep your ego in control and accept life. Otherwise, the ego will yearn for things and force you to go to work for it, to buy it stuff to make it feel better.

Once you are at one with yourself, you'll have compassion for your Self. Then you will, of course, nurture yourself. But you won't have to go shopping to distract you from your fears. As you become more aware, you become more real. Then by discarding the useless stuff and eliminating unnecessary obligations, you become more balanced and settled, more silent and less manic. You'll have less activity and stress, and you'll feel better...and so onwards and upwards.

Do something for yourself every day, something compassionate and kind. I don't mean buying yourself breakfast; I mean doing something that is spiritually or physically nurturing: a massage, a fast, a meditation, exercise, rest, play—that kind of thing. For it's in the quiet time that you'll see the great abundance of this life, and you'll move from the ego's disquiet to the spirit's wholeness, and you'll see that the things you worry about are often not worth the worry. In the quiet time, you'll see what has real worth for you and what is just fluff and hype.

Once you get real, all your energy can go toward becoming what you really need and want to become. That transformation must be a part of your story in this lifetime. Making money is not enough—you will have to do something that has meaning.

You will want to collect memories in abundant settings, but you will also want to be surrounded by love and friendship; you will want to be doing things that you *want* to do.

Yes, that's your story. Put aside the little nit-picky ego stuff; start today to act, invoke, and energize the Grand Plan, for it is yours by right. All you have to do is agree to step up and collect. So accept yourself, and believe in yourself. Look the world in the eye and say, "I am what I am, and by the way, that'll be 30,000 bucks. Thank you."

—ɯ—

About the Author

Author and lecturer **Stuart Wilde** is one of the real characters of the self-help, human-potential movement. His style is humorous, controversial, poignant, and transformational. He has written numerous books, including those that make up the very successful Taos Quintet, which are considered classics in their genre. They are: *Affirmations, The Force, Miracles, The Quickening,* and *The Trick to Money Is Having Some.* Stuart's books have been translated into 12 languages.

Website: **www.stuartwilde.com**

❧ Notes ❧

❖ Notes ❖

❧ Notes ❧

❦ Notes ❦

❈ Notes ❈

✤ Notes ✤

❦ Notes ❦